# A GUIDE
*to the*
## H I S T O R I C
*French Quarter*

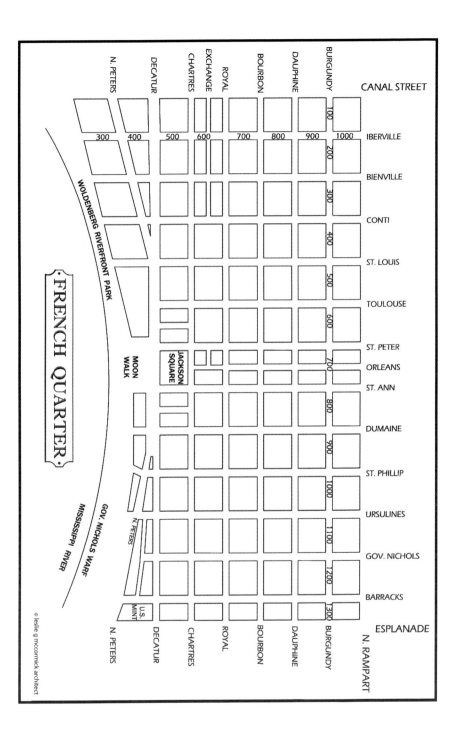

# A GUIDE
## *to the*
# HISTORIC
# *French Quarter*

ANDY PETER ANTIPPAS

THE
History
PRESS

Published by The History Press
Charleston, SC 29403
www.historypress.net

Copyright © 2013 by Andy Peter Antippas
All rights reserved

*Front cover*: Balcony. *Jorge de la Torriente.*

*Back cover*: Antoine's Restaurant. *Michael Bentley*; *middle, top*: Robert English. The
Cabildo, New Orleans (LA); Washington Artillery Park, Civil War cannon. *By
Flickr user jared422_80.*

First published 2013

Manufactured in the United States

ISBN 978.1.62619.280.5

Library of Congress Cataloging-in-Publication Data

Antippas, Andy Peter.
A Guide to the Historic French Quarter / Andy Peter Antippas.
pages cm
Includes bibliographical references and index.
ISBN 978-1-62619-280-5
1. Vieux Carré (New Orleans, La.)--Guidebooks. 2. New Orleans (La.)--
Guidebooks. 3. Historic buildings--Louisiana--New Orleans--Guidebooks. 4.
Vieux Carré (New Orleans, La.)--History. 5. New Orleans (La.)--History. I. Title.
F379.N56V526 2013
976.3'35--dc23
2013040246

*For my wife, Tricia Moss, and her tireless assistance, and for my two daughters, Athena and Artemis, who grew up strolling through the French Quarter with me almost every Sunday—pilgrimages always topped off by Swensen's Bubble Gum ice cream enjoyed while sitting among the pigeons in Jackson Square.*

# Contents

# Preface

L e Corbusier's eloquent injunction holds true for New Orleans: "Towns are born, and grow throughout the ages; they deform under the assaults of life." The French Quarter has been lived in and died in; human energy has been manifested continuously and freely for 250 years. Where we find presently a sedate restaurant, we would have found—20 years ago, 50 years ago, 100 years ago or more—a dry goods store, a grocery, a saloon, a coffeehouse, a patisserie, an apothecary, a gambling joint, a silversmith, a printer, a jeweler, a letter-writer, a whorehouse, a bank. They may have disappeared along with their proprietors, but they've left behind an aura that infuses the atmosphere.

It is this display of the deep and wide diversity of human lives, values and activities that is the greatness of the French Quarter and manifests itself in the range of its architectural styles, from the spectacular to the humble; its floral bouquet, from the overwhelming sweet olive behind the cathedral to the simple fern growing everywhere out of the moldering brick; in its restaurants, from the lowly shrimp po' boy and muffaletta to poulet sauce Rochambeau and poisson Meunière Amandine; and in its shops, from the grandest antique shops to the scruffiest T-shirt shop.

It would take Boccaccio, Dante, Chaucer or Balzac to capture the surge of diverse humanity that has continuously lived and paraded through the French Quarter, but everyone who visits the French Quarter will experience the subtle broadening of their own sensibilities—that increase in compassion and generosity that comes in the confrontation with the fullness of the created world and the varicolored experience of living.

Walking through the French Quarter there is a reassuring sense of fitness, of the coherence of space, of human proportions, where nothing steals sunshine. Nothing oppresses or impinges: the simple intricacy of the streets allows everything to open freely onto everything else. There is a miraculously perfect fusion of rigidity and fluidity intimately reflecting human, cope-able life. But it is not the "perfection" of a Williamsburg-style restoration that is the greatness of the French Quarter—indeed, it is the imminent possibility of decay that fills the French Quarter with romance.

Walking attentively through the Quarter enlarges the soul and encourages tolerance. Everything lives side-by-side in the French Quarter, the way Royal Street lives side-by-side with Bourbon Street, the way Ash Wednesday follows the debaucheries of Mardi Gras Tuesday. The French Quarter honors Saint Peter, Saint Ann and Saint Philip, and three other parallel streets commemorate Louis XIV's three bastard children, Conti, Toulouse and Dumaine. The French Quarter is un-condemning, un-embarrassed, filled with amused delight, buffoonery and the sacred, complex music of life—there is no place more interesting to stroll through.

# Acknowledgements

Indispensable for this undertaking were Francis Xavier Martin's *The History of Louisiana* (1821, reprinted 1963), John Kendall's *History of New Orleans* (1922), Grace King's *History of the Creole Families of New Orleans* (1921), Lyle Saxon's *WPA Guide to New Orleans* (1938) and the Louisiana Historical Association's ongoing "Dictionary of Louisiana Biography."

I am especially indebted to the charm, erudition and formidable notarial work of Stanley Clisby Arthur; the architectural and historical reference material provided in the work of Roulhac Toledano, Randolph Delehanty, Jim Fraiser and the editors of *The Esplanade Ridge, New Orleans Architecture*, Vol. V; the sense of place of Richard and Marina Campanella; and the Shorpies at the Shorpy Historical Photo Archive.

All the photographic material is courtesy of the Library of Congress, Prints and Photographs Division. The anonymous photographs from about 1880 to 1910 are from the LOC's Detroit Publishing Company Collection; the ones from the late 1930s are from the LOC's Carnegie Survey of the Architecture of the South archive. The Carnegie Corporation had the vision to give grants to Frances Benjamin Johnston to photograph nine southern states. Certainly, her photographs of dilapidated interiors and exteriors of structures in the French Quarter helped quicken the preservationist movement.

The map of the French Quarter is courtesy of Leslie McCormick, AIA, CNU, and Studio McCormick.

In the course of correcting the errors of others, I very likely made errors of my own—which I hope to correct (andy. antippas@gmail.com).

I deeply appreciate the patience, encouragement and advice of my History Press editors, Christen Thompson and Jaime Muehl.

# *A History of the French Quarter*

The mystery of the river the Indians called *misi sipi*, the "ancient father of waters," remained undisclosed despite the best efforts of the Spanish explorers of the early and middle sixteenth century. Even the direction of its flow was obscured into a legend that it divided the continent of North America from east to west. It was this legend that spurred René-Robert Cavelier, Sieur de La Salle, to explore the prospect of finding a route to China. After thirteen years of misery and exhaustion, he trekked down to the Gulf and, in 1682, raised the standard of France on the bank of the river, claiming the vast region lying east and west for his sovereign, the Sun King, Louis XIV, and naming it Louisiana.

La Salle's efforts to fortify and settle the present site of the French Quarter in 1684 and again in 1687 were futile, and it was only in 1697, when a momentary peace had come to war-ravaged France, that Count Louis de Pontchartrain, the French minister of the marine, could equip Pierre Le Moyne, Sieur d'Iberville, for another attempt. In 1698, Iberville sailed from Brest to Ship Island in the Gulf and, with barges laden with stores and munitions, continued up the tangled mouth of the river to the abandoned site on the crescent, where he reaffirmed France's claim.

Iberville's swashbuckling temperament led him to exhaust his supplies and his energies contending with the English and the Spanish settlements along the coast and trying to fortify Mobile. During his absence from the infant colony, he appointed as commander his younger brother from Montreal, Jean Baptiste Le Moyne, Sieur de Bienville. More organized and determined than his brother, Bienville successfully subdued and governed the Indians in the vicinity and settled fellow French-Canadians to test the soil and climate. When more provisions and men came in February 1718 under the financial auspices of John Law's Company of the West, the same ships carried back the announcement that the city on the crescent, between the river and the lake—the French Quarter—had been founded and named La Nouvelle-Orléans after the regent, the Duke of Orléans.

Some of the emigrant colonists came from France with anticipation and enthusiasm, some fleeing debtors and still others stolen from the back streets of Paris. Acadians came, Spaniards, slaves freighted up from the West Indies and Africa, the Ursuline sisters, Germans, Irish, Italians and other adventurous men from the rest of Europe—and the diversity of physiognomy and character that has continuously intrigued visitors to the French Quarter was firmly established.

All the while, the city's population was swelling. Bienville was busy with his engineer and architect, laying out the streets, fifty French feet apart, into the squares that now compose the *Vieux Carré*, the "Old Square," or the French Quarter. All early maps of the French Quarter testify to assistant engineer Adrien de Pauger's urban planning skills and extraordinary sense of place. The French had considerable experience in building frontier towns in the New World: Quebec in 1608, Montreal in 1642, Detroit in 1701 and Mobile in 1702. There are certain similarities among the early plans for these cities, but the French Quarter, far more than the others, is the product of the paradoxical French mind that always seems to vibrate between an academic neoclassicism and an uncontrollable romanticism. On the one hand, the logical formality of the French Quarter's chessboard pattern reflects the neoclassical urge to assert civilizing order against the savage wilderness; on the other hand, the romantic impulse is evident, as the square pattern appears to dissolve into a graceful curve following the flow of the river—the Crescent City.

For New Orleans, the grid was the only practical design. Bienville and Pauger assumed it would be easy to defend since it facilitated the movement of the small garrison to meet the emergencies created by the Natchez, Chickasaw and Choctaw Indians. But Bienville was always understaffed militarily, and in spite of all his and his successor's precautions, the city was always vulnerable to attack. If the grid pattern did not contribute much to the city's defenses, it did add immeasurably to the potential for civic growth by permitting an orderly, organically cellular expansion, laterally toward the lake and vertically along the river. The individual square blocks, interlaced with drainage ditches, were subdivided into ten or twelve lots with depths of 120 to 150 feet. There were separate and individually identifiable spaces forcefully, yet gently, integrated into a total unity. The proximity of the houses, the shared gardens, vines and shade are all marks of both French individualism and, eventually, Spanish gregariousness.

Almost fifteen years of intermittent war with the neighboring Indians, especially the Chickasaw and the Natchez, and disagreements with French government officials exhausted Bienville and obliged his return to France in 1743. The outbreak of war between the French and English for the possession of the Canadian territories brought an end to the first period of New Orleans' history.

In November 1762, with the signing of the Treaty of Paris, Louis XV ceded all French territories east of the Mississippi to England with the exception of the area around the French Quarter; however, a secret clause in the treaty, made public in October 1764, transferred the unexplored area west of the Mississippi River to Spain. When D'Abadie, the governor of New Orleans, at last informed the troubled citizens, they dispatched a mission to Paris to beg revocation of the treaty, but they were not received. In March 1767, Don Antonio D'Ulloa, the Spanish envoy, with two companies of infantry, came to take over the colony's administration in the name of King Carlos III. In great consternation, the citizens of New Orleans and the surrounding areas met and ordered D'Ulloa to make public his credentials of authority. Irritated that the dignity of his king should be called to account by a civil tribunal, D'Ulloa indignantly departed.

The Spanish government's response to the colony's "seditious" action was to order into the area Don Alejandro O'Reilly, lieutenant general of the armies of Spain, with a large force of troops and twenty-four ships. In August 1769, O'Reilly entered the city and, with ceremonious arrogance, presented his documents of authority. The French flag was lowered and the Spanish dominion began. Almost immediately, the "conspirators" responsible for the expulsion of D'Ulloa, among them representatives of the noblest French families, were transported to dungeons in Havana or bayoneted or shot and their property confiscated.

The hostility toward the Spanish was soon considerably mitigated under the benign stewardships of Don Luis de Aurenzaga, Bernardo de Galvez and Don Esteban de Miró. It was under Miró's command that the hideous fire that destroyed the heart of the French Quarter occurred. It began on Good Friday, March 21, 1788, on Chartres near St. Louis. According to Governor Miró's report, 356 buildings were destroyed. When Miró retired to Spain, he was replaced by Baron François Louis Hector de Carondelet, formerly the governor of San Salvador in Guatemala. In addition to rebuilding the city still in ruins, Carondelet had to confront, more directly than any former governor, precisely what relationship was to be established between New Orleans and the new American nation to the east. Already pioneers had begun to settle in the area, flatboats were a frequent sight in the harbor and the levees bustled with merchant Yankees. The most notorious exportation of the Americans, however, was the spirit of revolution.

The ideals of the American Revolution had already ignited all of France. Louis XVI had been executed, a republic proclaimed and war declared against Spain. The Frenchmen in New Orleans immediately rallied to the new government in Paris, and Carondelet was obliged to strengthen the Spanish claim on the city with militia and fortifications. The governors who followed—Gayoso de Lemos, Don Francisco Bouligny, Sebastián de Casa Calvo and especially Brigadier General Don Juan Manuel de Salcedo—continued the attempts to suppress the city's revolutionary spirit and curtail American participation in the economic life of the province. In the fall of 1802, a decree was passed prohibiting Americans from depositing their goods at the port for transshipment.

News slowly reached the city that Napoleon had, in effect, successfully fully reannexed Louisiana from Spain by the Treaty of San Ildefonso negotiated on October 1, 1800. When the French prefect Pierre Clément Laussat landed at New Orleans, he was greeted with wild rejoicings, and preparations were made for the transfer. However, diplomatic arrangements between President Jefferson and Napoleon made the raising of the French tricolor over the city less than a mere formality. The United States had already purchased New Orleans and one million square miles of territory in the very heartland of the continent for $15 million on April 30, 1803.

On December 20, American commissioners General James Wilkinson and William Claiborne, who was soon to be appointed governor, arrived in New Orleans and accepted the keys to the city. The period of transition was by no means peaceful. The administrators spoke neither French nor Spanish, and they naturally chose their civil staff from other Americans, causing considerable rancor, jealousy and distrust among the rest of the inhabitants. Of greatest concern among the predominantly Catholic New Orleanians was the prospect that the Protestant Americans would expel the few remaining Ursuline sisters and confiscate their property. Only a letter sent from President Jefferson allayed their fears. The line dividing the population was clearly demarcated when, after the city's incorporation in 1806, virtually no one among the Creoles (those of the Spanish and French families) exercised the privilege of voting for their aldermen. Voting was, after all, strictly an Americanism.

One event, however, effaced the lines between the American, Spanish, French and all the other diverse citizenry forever: the British attack on New Orleans. It is not too much to say that without the personal genius of Major General Andrew Jackson, New Orleans would have been destroyed, the Louisiana territory claimed by the English and the entire history of the North American continent altered.

The situation was perilous. The city's naval and land defenses were poorly equipped, and the neighboring southern states were too sparsely settled to offer any assistance. Washington, and the capitol itself, had been successfully routed and burned by the British forces in August and the federal government considerably weakened; furthermore, the city's spirit was undermined by the ambiguous allegiances of its citizens. Not unmindful of the seriousness of the matter, Jackson knew that a decisive show of American military enterprise was essential to arouse the pride and confidence of the New Orleanians. The opportunity came quickly. Four British ships, with ninety guns and six hundred marines, sailed against Fort Bowyer in Mobile Bay seeking a base from which to launch their attack on New Orleans. Jackson so perfectly organized and inspired the handful of men defending the fort that they successfully repelled the British assault on September 15, 1814. With equally impressive skill, Jackson subsequently attacked and took Pensacola on November 7, 1814, forestalling any designs the Spanish might have had on helping the British.

Jackson's courage was infectious. By the time he returned to New Orleans on December 2, the city was spilling over with patriotic zeal and an army was assembling, the likes of which America had never seen before: French and Spanish planters, merchants and clerks from the French Quarter, Tennessee militia, vital Kentucky regulars, a cavalry troop from Mississippi, Creole militia, two companies of freed slaves, one hundred Choctaw braves and Jean and Pierre Lafitte's Baratarian pirate-patriots. Jackson acted decisively when he learned of the British maneuvering at the entrance to Lake Pontchartrain and their advance through the marshes to within six or seven miles south of the French Quarter. Jackson proceeded with his forces to the Rodriguez Canal, where they entrenched themselves some two miles from the British camp on Chalmette Plain.

That night, on December 23, Jackson sent a cavalry troop to harass the English and directed Master Commandant Daniel T. Patterson to move the fourteen-gun *Carolina* downriver. Unsettled by the impudent cavalry foray, the British were caught by surprise as the *Carolina*'s cannon devastated their camp with grapeshot. Almost simultaneously, Jackson's infantry attacked both British flanks, compounding their disorder. Jackson and his men withdrew to the Rodriguez Canal and spent that night and the next fortifying the ditch's embankment with cotton bales and timber. The British, meanwhile, spent that night and the next day suffering broadsides from the *Louisiana* as well as the *Carolina*. They could draw solace from the arrival of the vast part of their army and artillery slowly trickling in from the marshes, and they could anticipate the arrival, on Christmas Day, of their commander in chief, the brother-in-law of the Duke of Wellington, Sir Edward Pakenham.

Pakenham wasted no time. He deliberated with his staff and mobilized his disheartened troops. He ordered all artillery available mounted on the levee and directed against the *Carolina* and the *Louisiana*. On the night of the twenty-sixth, the British battery demolished the *Carolina* and compelled the *Louisiana* to retreat to the American line of defense. The next morning, Pakenham advanced across Chalmette Plain. On his right was Gibb's column, on his left was Keane's column and in skirmish line between them was a crack rifle brigade.

The British commander had reason to feel confident: he was bringing more than 8,000 war-hardened veterans who had fought Napoleon to bear against fewer than 2,600 irregulars. He must have been rudely jarred when the Baratarian pirates, under the command of Dominique You, opened up with their cannons and decimated Keane's troops, as well as when Gibbs was routed by unending musket fire from the ramparts. His flanks virtually destroyed, Pakenham retreated. Sir Alexander Cochrane, vice admiral of the British fleet gathered on Lake Borgne, argued that they should bring in artillery from the fleet to breech the American fortifications, and by the evening of January 31, the British had established three rows of artillery within four hundred yards of the American position. The next morning, there was a violent exchange of cannonades, and the British guns were destroyed.

Pakenham had one more plan born out of frustration: to outflank Jackson on the opposite bank and to attack in a massive head-on assault. By January 8, the day of the final encounter, both sides had received reinforcements, and the Americans and the British numbered approximately five thousand and ten thousand, respectively.

The resulting engagement on January 8, 1815, was terrible in its destruction. Amidst confusion, Gibbs attacked on the left, and Keane moved forward on the right. Gibbs and his column were cut to pieces by the Tennesseans and freshly arrived Kentuckians firing deadly volleys into his ranks. Gibbs was mortally wounded, and Pakenham, coming to relieve his position, was himself killed by a charge of grapeshot. Keane was killed on the other side of the battlefield. The British retreated, exhausted and defeated, across Chalmette Plain and returned to their ships. Although accounts vary, it is estimated that in the entire campaign against New Orleans, more than two thousand British died; the Americans lost fewer than two hundred. Jackson returned to the city and was accorded a hero's welcome for his magnificent achievement. The only consolation for the British troops was that they returned to England, joined up with the Duke of Wellington and helped defeat Napoleon at Waterloo, five months later, on June 18, 1815.

Over the next decades, the city grew at an extraordinary rate. Canals were filled in and made into boulevards; many of the plantations, such as the Marigny, De Bore, Foucher and Lafreniere estates, were divided up into streets and the dock and warehouse facilities enlarged to handle the barges and steamboats. The dazzling future of the city had an ominous specter hanging over it, however: the seemingly unconquerable yellow fever and cholera epidemics.

Although outbreaks occurred with deadly regularity throughout the history of the colony, particularly devastating plagues befell the city in the early 1830s and the late 1840s, causing the deaths of tens of thousands—between 1793 and 1905, over 100,000 died of cholera, malaria, yellow fever and dysentery. But the energy of the growing city, as mighty as the river that flowed at its side, withstood every onslaught, and in the midst of hardship and deprivation, New Orleans struggled to define itself. There were better hotels, more opera, more flamboyant Mardi Gras celebrations and a diversity of new life to replenish the old.

While the destructive fires of 1788 and 1794 or the yellow fever epidemics could not bring the city to its knees, slavery—more pernicious—succeeded. Rightfully or wrongfully, but nonetheless chivalrously, New Orleans gave its resources in defense of the

"Good Friday in front of old St. Louis cathedral, c. 1910." It was on Good Friday, March 21, 1788, when badly placed devotional candles at 619 Chartres Street resulted in a fire that destroyed about four hundred buildings in the French Quarter. *Library of Congress.*

Confederacy and neglected its own fortifications. On January 26, 1861, Flag Officer Farragut, with seventeen gunboats, sailed virtually unopposed past the ineffectual shore batteries positioned at the mouth of the river and, on April 25, 1862, took New Orleans. The citizenry were humiliated at their defeat, at the threats to bombard the city and at the tearing down of the state flag. Nothing could compare, however, with the indignation they reserved for the provost marshal, General "Beast" Butler. He imprisoned everyone in sight for the most absurd infractions of the law, caused New Orleans women to be branded streetwalkers if they were rude to his troops and confiscated property and had it auctioned at a miserable, if any, return to the owners.

Things were not much improved when General Banks took over as commander in December. The spirit of New Orleans lay trembling and nearly crushed. The brooding resentment exploded in unbridled violence in 1867. In that year, the federal government's troops enforced its attempts at Reconstruction throughout the South.

In 1874, elections were called in an attempt to clarify the confusion resulting from the rival claims of the Republicans and the Liberal Republican-Democrats to the governorship and the state legislature. In order to prevent their disenfranchisement by the federal militia, the New Orleanians formed the White League. On September 14, 1874, a company of leaguers stormed the militia's barricades at the levee, and another league company assaulted the batteries formed in front of the customhouse. Both attacks were successful and the militia routed.

President Grant sent troops to preserve the Republican government, but when the elections were finally held, the Democrats won. It was not until the elections of 1876, however, and President Rutherford B. Hayes's withdrawal of support from the carpetbaggers, that the burden of Reconstruction was lifted and New Orleans was once again in the hands of those who loved it most: its citizens. Within a few years, the University of Louisiana was reopened, and the Mississippi River Commission was formed to reorganize the levee building and to bring flooding under control. The mouth of the river was opened to the ships of the world, and recognition of New Orleans' growing importance within the economy of the United States was affirmed when the International Cotton Centennial Exposition was held in Audubon Park in 1884.

The history of New Orleans thereafter is the history of the vicissitudes of the other great cities of the United States—but with a significant difference. Perhaps more than those other cities, the romance of the ancient days, pervasive and animating, gave stability to the flux and strain of the city's growth. From 1890 through the 1930s, other parts of the city grew and stabilized, but the French Quarter, as many of the photographs from that period in this volume will show, was threatened with extinction. Hurricanes and fires were not the only enemies; there was also pervasive decay from the damp weather, the blight brought on by tenement living and abandonment (families simply moved out). First it was the writers and painters who came for inexpensive studio space in the 1920s, and then the great far-sighted preservationists and architects and

"Grand Army of the Republic Monument, c. 1910." There are few southern cities generous enough to permit a monument to fallen Union soldiers. It was erected by Union veterans in 1874 and is across the field from the site of the Battle of New Orleans at Chalmette National Historical Park. The Latin inscription reads: "Though they are silent, they cry aloud." *Library of Congress.*

the civic-minded businessmen stepped forward—the Arts and Crafts Club, the Vieux Carré Commission, Richard Koch, Leonard Huber, Stanley Clisby Arthur, Clay Shaw and Elizabeth Werlein (who founded the Vieux Carré Property Owners Association), to mention only a few—followed by the present-day organizations, like the Friends of the Cabildo, that continue the battle. In 2005, while the fury of Katrina and the ensuing flooding caused much of the city merciless wreckage, the French Quarter stood solidly above the destruction. An enchantment so natural seems inextinguishable, so imbued into masonry and brick that nothing could destroy it. With civic progress swirling around it, the French Quarter, the organic nucleus of the city, tattered and abused, miraculously survives.

# CHAPTER 1

# Royal Street

## THE GATEWAY INTO THE FRENCH QUARTER

The most appropriate place to begin our stroll into the French Quarter is at the corner of Canal Street and Royal. In the early part of the twentieth century, this corner of Canal and Royal was called the "Monkey Wrench Corner"—where unemployed seaman (monkeys) would gather in hopes of borrowing money (wrenching) for food and lodging from their employed friends. In 1825, unlike the rest of the French Quarter (the *Vieux Carré*, the "Old Quarter"), most of Royal Street was already paved with discarded ships' ballast—everything outside the French Quarter was a quagmire green with weeds, rushes and palmetto. By the 1840s, Royal Street was confirmed as the main shopping and business locale, renowned for its banking institutions, hotels, cafés, shops and elegant residences, where many of the leading families lived. The street's architecture today is practically the same as it was then—a synthesis of Spanish, French and American. The charming irregularity of the old buildings, the balconies hung with lacy iron, the stately doorways and archways barely hiding patios and courtyards festooned with camellias, magnolias, heliotrope and jasmine all confirm the city's historical continuum.

Details about the unsurpassed architectural richness of the French Quarter are important, of course, but of equal interest are the businesses and the fascinating residents who inhabited the buildings. Almost every street in the French Quarter can boast compelling and sometimes bizarre stories of the men and women who shaped the complex texture of the French Quarter, and they will be noted on the itinerary. Some of the addresses have changed over the years or the buildings have been demolished or altered, but in the magical ambiance of the French Quarter, their ghosts persist.

Keep in mind, the numbers on the right, or the river side, are even; on the left, or the lake (Ponchartrain) side, they are odd. Each block is numbered in units of 100. (For example, the "200 Block" is the second block down from Canal.)

## 100 ROYAL (1833)

This building was the first in the city constructed of northern granite instead of the ballast stone from English trading vessels.

## 103 ROYAL, "SMALLEST NEWS AND POSTCARD STAND" (1908)

Mr. Wallace might have had a tiny newsstand, but his offerings were wide ranging. In addition to all the New Orleans postcard scenes, he covered entertainment with the *Dramatic Mirror*, *Billboard*, *Variety*, *Show World* and *Stageland* and pulp fiction with the *Blue Book Magazine* (Agatha Christie, Edgar Rice Burroughs and Zane Gray). In the accompanying image, tucked between the postcard racks to Mr. Wallace's left is the *Sagebrush Philosopher*, a monthly published by M.C. "Bill" Barrow, a Wyoming writer read nationwide for his wit ("Live, laugh, love—there'll be a time when you can't"). The *Saturday Evening Post* in the corner is dated June 13, 1908. The *Chicago Tribune* cover features William Howard Taft, who had been nominated that week at the Republican

"Smallest news and post card stand, 103 Royal Street, c. 1900–1915." *Library of Congress.*

Convention held in Chicago. The etched door window in the back reads, "The Jewel," an oyster bar located at 131 Royal. The tile insert on the street also reads, "The Jewel Café."

## 106 ROYAL (CIRCA 1800)

The home of M.E.M. Davis served as Andrew Jackson's headquarters in December 1814. This is where he planned his defense of New Orleans against the imminent attack of the British.

"Court yard of the home of Mrs. M.E.M. Davis," 106 Royal Street, which served as Jackson's headquarters in 1814. Photo c. 1901. *Library of Congress.*

## 121 ROYAL (CIRCA 1830S)

Dr. Francisco Antommarchi, the Corsican physician who attended Napoleon during his exile at St. Helena, displayed the emperor's death mask in the building that formerly occupied this site.

## 126 ROYAL (1836), THE MERCHANT'S EXCHANGE

The ground floor was the U.S. Post Office in 1842; the second floor was strictly for business transactions until 1845, when it became the U.S. District Court. After the Civil War, the entire building became a gambling casino renowned throughout the United States as "Number 18 Royal Street."

"Royal Street from Canal, c. 1906," 100 block of Royal Street. The original columned Union Bank/casino stood where Walgreen's is now located. The street banner advertises Lawrence Fabacher's Oyster Bar, which was at 137 Royal Street. Fabacher later founded the famous Jax Brewery. The Commercial Hotel on the next corner was eventually absorbed by the prestigious Monteleone Hotel in 1908. *Library of Congress.*

## 140 ROYAL (1832)

The original building on the corner, rebuilt in 1948, now occupied by a drugstore, was designed by Jacques Nichols and Joseph Isadore de Pouilly for the Union Bank of Louisiana. It, too, became a gambling hall soon after the bank collapsed in 1849.

When the definitive history of gambling in the United States is written, it will document the fact that Las Vegas had its schooling in the casinos of New Orleans, which have shady traditions well back into the nineteenth century. The high point of gambling in New Orleans, however, was between 1938 and 1953. The queen of the casinos was the Jai Lai Club on Friscoville in old Arabi, in the Lower Ninth Ward. All of the New Orleans clubs were closed by the Kefauver hearings in 1953. Bugsy Segal opened Las Vegas in 1954.

"French Quarter Milk Delivery, c. 1903." A milk car delivering to the Hotel and Restaurant de la Louisiane, founded in 1881, located at 719 Iberville. Adam Schoendor, whose name is on the cart, owned Hunter's Dairy at Ne Plus Ultra Street (now Lafrenière) and Havana Streets outside the Quarter. The horse has a harness with "A" and "S' worked into the medallions. *Library of Congress.*

"Old Absinthe House, the bar," 238–40 Bourbon Street, c. 1900–1906. Inside are two absinthe fountains from which iced water drizzled onto a slowly dissolving sugar lump in a slotted spoon over the glass of absinthe, which then *louches*— turns milky. Three parts water to one part absinthe was traditional. It is said that sawdust on the floor made it easier to sweep up blood from the inevitable fights breaking out among those indulging in the "Green Fairy." *Library of Congress.*

SIDE STROLL: Take a left on the corner of the 200 block and go down Bienville Street one block to Bourbon Street. On the corner is the Old Absinthe House (238–40 Bourbon, 1806), where the likes of Aaron Burr, Oscar Wilde and Aleister Crowley sipped glasses of absinthe, or the "Green Fairy," locally distilled, until it was banned nationwide in 1912 by the federal government. Two of New Orleans' most venerable restaurants are within a half a block: Galatoire's (209 Bourbon) and Arnaud's (813 Bienville).

## 214 AND 217–23 ROYAL

The photo in this section must have actually been taken in the first week of 1908. The Monteleone Hotel (214 Royal Street) on the left just opened, and the furniture store across the street (217–223), owned by W.G. Tebault, burned to the ground on January 7, 1908. Despite numerous fires in his furniture stores, Mr. Tebault was dubbed the "King of Royal Street." The mysterious Bactrian two-humped camel cutout suspended over the street is possibly announcing a circus event. Camels were a big attraction for circuses and often hauled the animal cage wagons when the circuses paraded through town. Camels summoned up the exotic, romantic spirit of Turkey, Egypt and the whole unknown Middle East. For this reason, in 1913, R.J. Reynolds chose a dromedary, the Arabian single-humped camel, as his cigarette logo. The Bactrian variety from central Asia was still a novelty. In 1855, when Jefferson Davis was U.S. secretary of war, he commissioned a ship to bring in camels for the army to use in Texas and the Southwest because the mules

"Royal St., Looking toward Canal St., c. 1910." *Library of Congress.*

and horses couldn't survive the arid countryside. That first load carried thirty-three dromedaries and only two Bactrians. It wasn't until 1870 that Dan Castello's Great Circus and Egyptian Caravan introduced audiences to the two-humped variety.

For 1908, *Billboard* lists three tent events in New Orleans—Ringling Bros. and the Gentry Bros.—but both were later that year. The third was a show by New Orleans impresario Signor Faranta, aka Frederick William Stemple, a vaudevillian, contortionist, showman and Elk, who apparently had a traveling circus troupe as early as 1895 and regularly acquired animals at auction from bankrupt circuses. For example, according to *Wisconsin Week* of November 25, 1886, when W.W. Cole's circus went to auction in New Orleans on November 11, Faranta acquired four elephants ($7,150), a "white buffalo yak" ($200), three lions ($824), two white peacocks ($28) and a female Hippo ($1,500). Out of corrugated metal, in 1884, Faranta built something called the "Iron Building," for which there appears to be no extant illustration and virtually no documentation, although it is alleged to have held five thousand patrons. It was located prominently on the corner of Orleans and Bourbon Streets, much to the consternation of the black Order of Nuns, the Sisters of the Holy Family, which had just taken over the building next door, where the Quadroon Balls were held (although they did lease the space to him). The Iron Building is variously referred to as Faranta's Amphitheater, Pavilion or Circus. Since posters had always been the way circuses heralded their comings, hanging a huge cutout on Royal Street was a novelty and could have been pulled off only by someone well known in the community.

## 240 ROYAL STREET (CIRCA 1798)

This plastered brick building (actually two contiguous structures) was purchased by Fanchonette Robert, a free woman of color, in 1799 and is in an excellent state of preservation. New Orleans bricks were made from the sandy clay of the Mississippi and the mortar from burning clamshells. The mortar proved more stable than the crumbling brick, and it was often necessary to plaster over the exteriors.

## 301–05–07 ROYAL (1838)

Between 1841 and 1860, these were the showrooms and workshops of Prudent Mallard, born in Sèvres, France, and one of New Orleans' greatest furniture designers in mahogany and rosewood. From 1924 to 1935(?), E. Hoffman Price, the California-born master SyFy, fantasy, horror, crime and adventure pulp magazine writer, lived at 305 Royal with his family and worked for Union Carbide. Writing in his spare time, he published his first story, many of which were set in the French Quarter's "dimly lit streets." Later, by June 1932, already an established writer, H.P. Lovecraft came to visit with him and see the city. It is certain that they talked all night while eating hot chili—what is mythical is the story that Price took Lovecraft to a brothel, where some of the ladies turned out to be Lovecraft fans. Lovecraft set one of his most famous stories, "The Call of Cthulhu," in a swamp just outside the French Quarter.

## 312 ROYAL (CIRCA 1828)

In 1839, this was the home of John Slidell, U.S. senator from Louisiana and later commissioner for the Confederacy to England. In 1861, Slidell and another Confederate envoy were on their way to England and France to win support for the Confederate cause. Their ship, the *Trent*, although a neutral British vessel, was seized by a Union warship, and the two men were arrested, an event referred to as the Trent Affair. The British were angry and threatened to support the Confederacy. The men were released.

## 334 ROYAL (1826)

The architect of this exceptionally beautiful building with Ionic columns was Benjamin F. Fox on behalf of the Louisiana Bank. When the bank closed in 1871, it briefly served as an auction house until the city acquired it. Then it served as the Mortgage and Conveyance Office and, still later, as the local American Legion station. It has been renovated for the use of the New Orleans Eighth District Police Department.

## 339 ROYAL (1800)

Although at the outset it was built as the home for a senior judge of the Spanish court, this building housed numerous banking enterprises: the Planter's Bank in 1811, the Bank of America of Philadelphia in 1820 and the New Orleans Gas Light and Banking Company in 1836. It has been the Waldhorn family antique shop since 1881.

"Exchange Alley, c. 1906." *Library of Congress.*

SIDE STROLL: Take a right on Conti Street and walk halfway down the street to Exchange Alley (or Passage or Place). This passageway, extending all the way to Canal Street, was created in 1831 to provide a rear entrance to the Merchant's Exchange (126 Royal). Its chief claim to fame, however, resides in the fact that between 1830 and 1870, the alley was the location of the most illustrious dueling academies in New Orleans. In the mid-1850s, the greatest duelist was Don José Pepe Llulla, a protégé of the legendary master L'Aloutte. When L'Aloutte died, Llulla took over his academy in the alley. He was an expert with knife, saber, short sword, rapier and pistol and fought at least twenty-five personal duels and served as a second in one hundred more. He died at seventy-three and is buried at St. Vincent de Paul Cemetery #1 (alley 2, left front) on Louisa Street.

Exchange Alley has another, perhaps even more dubious distinction: Lee Harvey Oswald lived at 126 Exchange with his divorced mother when he was sixteen, in 1955–56. This first block off Canal Street was a crime-filled area then, with gambling joints run by Carlos Marcello and his Mafia.

## A NOTE ON DUELING

The volatile mixture of temperaments in New Orleans made it dangerous to argue politics at the coffee shop or step on someone's boot at the opera. Duels were fought for all manner of slights. Usually the contests took place at either St. Anthony's Garden, behind the cathedral, or at the Dueling Oaks. There is the great story of the Creole gentleman who overheard a visitor from Europe, a hydrologist, comment disparagingly on the Mississippi River, saying how insignificant it was compared to the great rivers of Europe. The Creole gentleman immediately stepped forward and slapped him in the face, demanding satisfaction at the Dueling Oaks in what is now City Park. The next morning, the European left the field of honor with a slashed and profusely bleeding cheek.

"Avenue under the oaks, old dueling grounds, c. 1910." City Park. *Library of Congress.*

In the early part of the nineteenth century, the Creoles, Spanish and French preferred the blade, and most fights were concluded with the infliction of even a minor wound. The combatants might drop their weapons, embrace and end up drinking buddies for life. However, when the Americans warmed up to dueling, they preferred pistols, rifles and, occasionally, shotguns, so the fatalities started to pile up. In 1855, the city tried to enforce the always existing, but always ignored, law against dueling, but it came to a natural halt during the Civil War. Still, it persisted later, until the 1880s. The last recorded duel occurred at the Oaks on June 22, 1889. When the first shots were fired, a policeman arrived and arrested both men. Of the two oaks lending the dueling grounds its name, one succumbed to disease and a hurricane, but the other survives. It is about three hundred years old and is located behind the New Orleans Museum of Art at the intersection of Dueling Oaks Drive and Dreyfous Drive. New Orleans City Park, the largest municipal park in the country, has the largest number of mature oaks in the world.

SIDE STROLL: Take a left on Conti. Across Bourbon Street is Broussard's Restaurant (819 Conti), and a block farther is Musée Conti Wax Museum (917 Conti), which has many bloody tableaus displaying scenes from French Quarter and Louisiana history, from the founding to the present, including Huey Long, Louis Armstrong and Napoleon in a tiny bathtub (it is said that Napoleon signed the Louisiana Purchase document while sitting in his marble tub; there are three existing marble bathtubs belonging to Napoleon: one in a private collection, one in the Louvre and one at Le Pavillon Hotel at 833 Poydras Street in New Orleans). There is also the obligatory monster room with Frankenstein and the Swamp Thing. (Wax Museum information, 504-525-2605)

## 400 ROYAL (1908–10)

From 1997 to 2004, this exceptional Beaux Arts white granite and marble courthouse building occupying the square block underwent a $20 million restoration and once again houses the Supreme Court of Louisiana, the Fourth Circuit Court of Appeals, the state judicial administrator, the Law Library of Louisiana and an office for the state attorney general. The monument in front is of Edward Douglass White (1844–1921), ninth chief justice of the U.S. Supreme Court, and is known as "Big Green Ed." It is said that if you circle the statue counterclockwise a few times, no matter how badly you have misbehaved in the French Quarter that night you will not be arrested.

"Royal Street from the court house, c. 1910[?]," *Library of Congress.*

## 401 ROYAL (1821)

Formerly the Louisiana State Bank—note the bank's monogram on the wrought-iron balcony—this building was designed in 1820 by Benjamin Latrobe, the architect of the White House's South Wing. He died in the yellow fever epidemic and didn't live to see the building's completion.

## 413 ROYAL (1807)

Dominique Rouquette, whose initials appear on the balcony railing, was a wealthy importer of wines from Bordeaux and the first owner of this building. The architect was François du Jarreau, who also designed and built the adjoining building at 409 Royal in the same year. His son, Adrien Emmanuel Rouquette, was educated in Nantes, France. Rouquette gave up the practice of law to become a hermit missionary among the Choctaw Indians, living in the forests of St. Tammany Parish until his death in 1887. He was so revered that the Choctaw called him *Chata Ima*—"Like a Choctaw." He was an accomplished poet in French and English and met with Walt Whitman in 1875.

## 417 ROYAL (CIRCA 1801), THE "PATIO ROYAL" (A BRENNAN'S PROPERTY SINCE 1955)

This structure was built by Don José Faurie. In 1805, he sold it to Julian Poydras, the president of the Louisiana Bank, chartered in 1804 by Governor W.C.C. Claiborne as the first bank in the territory of the Louisiana Purchase. The railing on the balcony, with its beautiful supporting brackets, bears the bank's monogram in three places. In 1819, when the bank's charter expired, the building was sold to Martin Gordon and later, in 1841, to Judge Alonzo Morphy (the name was originally Murphy), father of Paul Morphy, the chess prodigy. Young Morphy learned to play watching his father and uncle. In 1850, at the age of twelve, he defeated a visiting Hungarian champion three times. He received his law degree but at nineteen was too young to practice, so he went to New York City to play chess at the First American Chess Congress, where he defeated everyone. When he traveled to Europe to find opponents, the English champion avoided him, offering lame excuses. Morphy then went to Paris and defeated the strongest French player and a visiting German champion as well. Between 1858 and 1862, he was regarded as the world's best player. He eventually developed an aversion for chess, and especially for chess players, and retired from competition. He became somewhat mentally unstable the last ten years of his life—the *New York Sun*'s obituary said it was from all the blindfolded games he played. He died in this building at the age of forty-seven of "apoplexy"; that is, a stroke. He is buried in New Orleans at St. Louis Cemetery No. 1, tomb 366. Visitors to his family tomb leave chess pieces behind in homage to one of greatest chess masters who ever lived.

"345 Royal [441 Royal Street], 1937–1938." *Library of Congress.*

## 437 ROYAL (1800)

This structure is particularly famous for accommodating Antoine Peychaud's apothecary. From his native Santo Domingo, Peychaud brought with him special bitters, which he added to cognac and served to his customers in an egg-shaped cup called a *coquetier* (or he used the cup to measure out the bitters and cognac). In any case, *coquetier* eventually became "cocktail."

## 441 ROYAL STREET (CIRCA 1800

Sicilian immigrant Louis Tortorichi founded this corner café and restaurant in 1900. Jax Beer began in 1913 in Jacksonville, Florida. In 1956, it sold its copyright to the New Orleans brewhouse on the Mississippi River across from Jackson Square, founded in 1891, which was, judging from the accompanying photograph, already

SIDE STROLL: At the end of the 400 block, take a left on St Louis. At 713–17 St. Louis is Antoine's Restaurant, the longest-running single-family-owned restaurant in the United States and still the queen of New Orleans restaurants. Farther, across Bourbon Street, is the Hermann-Grima Historic House Museum (818–20 St. Louis, 1831). Samuel Hermann, a German-Jewish immigrant merchant and cotton plantation owner, commissioned William Brand to design this Federal-style mansion for his family's home in 1831. A financial reverse during the national fiscal panic of 1837 obliged him to sell the house. Judge Felix Grima acquired it in 1844, and it remained in his family until 1924. The Women's Christian Exchange bought it in 1924 and used it as a boardinghouse for young women. The Exchange opened it as a museum in 1965, and the stables, which Grima added, serve as the museum shop, where the artwork of local female artists is sold today. The interior rooms re-create the elegant lifestyle of a wealthy family from 1830 to 1869. Most of the furnishings and accessories represent both families (Hermann and Grima) with additional period pieces. There are cooking demonstrations in the courtyard with the 1830s open-hearth stove (mostly on Thursdays). In October, the docents change the house decor and create the atmosphere of a family in mourning. The mood is lightened in December with festive Christmas decor and dessert treats. (Hermann-Grima House information, 504-525-5661).

A bit farther down, at 826–830 St Louis (1820), is what some believe to be the "House of the Rising Sun," the French Quarter house of ill-repute made famous by *The Animals* in 1964. The house may, in fact, be completely fictitious or possibly refer to a women's prison, a hotel or a syphilis hospital for prostitutes, all of which have been suggested. If it was a brothel, the best candidate is at this address on St. Louis, where, during an extensive renovation, risqué photos of semi-nude women and a ceiling mural depicting a rising sun flanked by cherubs were uncovered. Tradition holds that the madam was Marianne le Soleil Levant, whose name translates to "the eastern sun," ie, the "Rising Sun."

brewing or distributing a Jax Beer. In 1974, Jax Brewery went bankrupt, and the brand was acquired by the Pearl Brewing Co. in San Antonio, Texas. The Jax building is now a shopping mall with a second-floor museum devoted to the history of Jax beer.

SIDE STROLL: Return to Royal Street and walk to the right down St. Louis to Chartres Street. On the corner, directly across the street, is the original Maspero's Slave Exchange coffee and toddy shop (440 Chartres, 1788). In the early 1800s, this was the gathering place for everyone interested in news from abroad or in handling commercial transactions involving slaves or stolen pirate's booty. Jackson, his officers and Lafitte planned the defense of New Orleans on the second floor of this building—although some say that meeting was held on the second floor of the Old Absinthe House or at Mrs. Davis's home at 106 Royal Street.

"Chartres Street, c. 1906." The 500 block with the cathedral and the Cabildo in the distance. The archway on the left was part of the former St. Louis Hotel, now the Omni Royal Hotel. The Napoleon House, not visible, is on the corner right, and down the street, at 516 Chartres, was the location of Duflho's Pharmacy, now the Pharmacy Museum. *Library of Congress.*

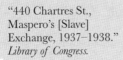

"440 Chartres St., Maspero's [Slave] Exchange, 1937–1938." *Library of Congress.*

## 500 Chartres Street (circa 1798), Girod House/Napoleon House Bar and Café

On the opposite corner from Maspero's Slave Exchange is the Girod House/Napoleon House Bar and Café (the second story and rooftop belvedere were added in 1814). It is traditionally held that Mayor Girod offered his home to Napoleon when Napoleon escaped from Elba or, alternately, that he and Dominique You, Lafitte's top lieutenant, plotted to rescue Napoleon after he was exiled to St. Helena and bring him to New Orleans. But before the plot could thicken, news came that Napoleon had died. The Impastato family has operated out of here since 1914. The engineer/architects, Laclotte and Latour, to whom the design is ascribed, smoothly merged both French and Spanish architectural elements, but it is still exceedingly French. The octagonal, copper-clad cupola on the steep-pitched hip roof is a

"The Napoleon House [500 Chartres Street], c. 1900–1906." *Library of Congress.*

"Girod House," Napoleon House, 500 Chartres Street, 1937–1938. *Library of Congress.*

landmark in the French Quarter. So, too, is the warm muffaletta and the Pimm's cup, which are here the order of the day.

## St. Louis Hotel

Directly across the street from the Napoleon House was the luxurious St. Louis Hotel, built in 1838 and demolished in 1915. It had a grand rotunda under which slave auctions occurred almost daily, between noon and three o'clock in the afternoon. Slave auctioneers like Maurice Barnett conducted their infamous business there. Barnett, who lived in Baton Rouge, was so engaged in the slave trade between 1840 and 1850 that he had an office in New Orleans and a permanent auction block at the St. Louis Hotel. He was a close associate of Jean Lafitte, who also trafficked in slaves. Barnett

himself "owned" eleven former citizens of Africa. The hotel fell into disrepair, became a haven for rats spreading plague and was torn down. The Omni Royal Hotel now occupies the site.

## 514 CHARTRES (1837), PHARMACY MUSEUM

The Pharmacy Museum is a detailed re-creation of the pharmacy of Louis Dufilho, who was born in France in 1787. He was a Sorbonne-educated chemist/pharmacist who came to New Orleans in 1803. In 1816, after a three-hour oral examination, he received his pharmacy license, the first issued in the United States. He practiced here from 1823 to 1850. The period mahogany cases on the first floor display early implements to administer drugs, a jar of live leeches, perfumes, belladonna laced tampons, bone saws and other surgical instruments shown alongside a necklace of garlic to ward off worms, gris-gris bags and voodoo love potions. There is plenty of Dr. Tichenor's Antiseptic, invented and bottled in New Orleans, and a soda fountain behind which sweet syrups, cocaine and alcohol fizzes were mixed to disguise the foul taste of some of the medicines. The second floor, where Dufilho and his wife, Emy, and their seven children lived, now houses Dr. J. William Rosenthal's spectacles collection. The courtyard in the back, with its medical herb gardens, is one of the few in the French Quarter where you can loiter and relax. Interestingly enough, when the city purchased the building, it was to be a museum devoted to Napoleon because it

*Opposite, top*: "La Tour and La Clotte's Atelier, 1937–1938," 625 Dauphine Street. In 1811, engineer/architects Arsène Lacarrière Latour and Jean Hyacinthe Laclotte took up studio residence here. Both studied at the Paris Academy of Fine Arts and designed significant buildings in the Quarter. Latour also devised the battlements behind which Jackson's men hunkered, and Laclotte served in the Battle of New Orleans as a private with the First Louisiana Militia. *Library of Congress.*

*Opposite, bottom*: "Old slave block in St. Louis Hotel, c.1900–1910." *Library of Congress.*

had been confused in the notarial records with the building on the corner. A Loyola University professor of pharmacy was the first to recognize the building's importance. The museum opened in 1950. (The Pharmacy Museum information, 504-565-8027).

## 522 CHARTRES (1803?)

This building was the home of Oliver Pollack, one of the least-acknowledged patriots of the Revolutionary War. An Irish merchantman from County Tyrone, he became one of the wealthiest men in the United States trading up and down the Mississippi Valley and abroad and operating his Tunica, Louisiana plantation. He personally contributed supplies and $300,000 (about $8 million in today's money) to the Revolutionary War effort—he was the largest individual monetary lender. As aide-de-camp, he also encouraged Governor Galvez, the representative of Spain in the territory, to engage and rout the British garrisons in Baton Rouge, Mobile and Pensacola. Pollock was the first to use the dollar sign. In his accountings to his friend Robert Morris in Pennsylvania, he continuously ran together the two letter abbreviation for Pesos, "ps"—Morris adopted "$" for official government use. Pollock ended up in debtor's prison in Cuba because he couldn't pay back the money he had borrowed from the Spanish government to lend to the colonial government. He was finally released and went to live with his daughter in Pinckneyville, Mississippi; eventually, President Jefferson was able to return some of the money owed him. His grave in Pinckneyville is unmarked, and there was never a likeness of him done.

*Back to Royal Street*

48

## 501 ROYAL (1806)

A few years after its completion, François Grandchamps ran his pharmacy in this building until 1842. John Vanderlyn, the first American painter to study in Paris and the portraitist of Washington and Madison, exhibited his paintings in New Orleans between 1821 and 1828. He painted portraits of wealthy planters in a studio above the pharmacy. The lacework on the balcony may be the first cast-iron grill decoration in the French Quarter. Cast-iron work came into favor around 1850, and much of it was designed and fabricated in New Orleans. Because of its higher carbon content, it is subject to rust and needs constant painting. The older wrought iron was probably also designed in New Orleans but very likely, at least early on, hand forged in Spain, probably near Seville, and transported from Cadiz to New Orleans.

## 519 ROYAL (1840?)

On the second floor of this building were the offices of E. Lorenz (Larry) Borenstein, who came to New Orleans in 1941 at the age of twenty-two, virtually penniless, from Milwaukee and ended up one of the largest property owners in the French Quarter. He was the bane of the preservationists because he loved the look of the decrepitude of his properties and would bring them up to code but refused to do anything but arrest the external decay. His theory of real estate "undevelopment" management can be seen at its best in Preservation Hall where the antique look is imperative to the ambiance. That space began as Borenstein's Associated Artists' Gallery, where he regularly invited out-of-work, older and forgotten musicians to jam in the evenings for tips. To formalize his support of the early jazz greats, he, along with Bill Russell and later Allan Jaffe, founded Preservation Hall at 726 St. Peter Street. At a time when segregation was still an issue in many southern cities, white and black musicians were able to play here side by side as they had in Storyville. Perhaps Borenstein's greatest contribution to the life of the French Quarter was his recognition and support of many "outsider" artists like Clementine Hunter, Sister Gertrude Morgan, Bruce Brice, Xavier de Callatay and, most importantly, Noel Rockmore, one of the great American painters of the last century, who drew his inspiration from the teeming and eccentric life of the French Quarter.

## 520 ROYAL (1816), SEIGNOURET-BRULATOUR BUILDING AND COURTYARD

This building was erected by François Seignouret, an importer of Bordeaux and even more famous as a designer of furniture. His initial (always on his furniture) makes up part of the wrought-iron *garde de frise* on the third floor intended to ensure the privacy of the balcony. The flagstone Brulatour Courtyard, one of the most beautiful in the French Quarter, takes its name from the late nineteenth-century owner of the building who ran his wine-importing business there from 1870 to 1887. A courtyard, in New Orleans terms, is much larger than a patio; is usually surrounded by high brick walls; has a fountain and small, orderly planting areas for flowers and herbs; and is almost always accessible from the street through a carriageway. The carriageway is often paved with flagstone or a stable herringbone brick pattern, usually three bricks deep to support the weight of a horse and carriage. The courtyard was used to receive visitors and deliveries and served as a workspace for ironmongers, to do laundry, to cook and to house the cisterns. A patio is usually enclosed by low walls of brick or, more often, wood, with the privacy enhanced by flowering trees and shrubs. It is always accessed only from the rear or side of the home.

In 1918, William R. Irby, a New Orleans philanthropist, restored the building and took up residence. He invited the early preservationist group the Arts and Crafts Club, which opened a gallery and art school downstairs in 1922. From 1949 to 1996, WDSU, New Orleans first TV station, had its offices and broadcast studios there. The Historic New Orleans Collection acquired the building in 2006.

"520 Royal Street, 1937–1938," the Brulatour courtyard. *Library of Congress.*

## 527–29–33 ROYAL (1792)

Don Francisco Merieult's home is one of the few to escape the fire of 1794 that destroyed more than two hundred houses and stores. His wife, Catherine McNamara, became a legend when she refused Napoleon's extravagant offers for her blond (some say red) hair, from which he wanted to make a wig for the Turkish sultan's favorite wife. Since 1974, the buildings at this address have contained the Historic New Orleans Collection Museum and Research Center. The complex of seven adjacent eighteenth- and nineteenth-century buildings was extensively remodeled in 1944–46 to house the collection of General and Mrs. Kemper Williams. At street level, in addition to the bookstore, the Williams Gallery has changing exhibits related to the cultural history of New Orleans. The ten rooms above are each devoted to a different period of New Orleans history. Tucked away in the back is the Williams's formerly private residence with antique and classic mid-twentieth-century furnishings. The research wing is located nearby at 410 Chartres Street. (HNOC information, 504-523-4662).

## 541 ROYAL (1798)

This building, also built by Merieult, is known as the "Court of Two Lions"—the entrance to the building, just around the corner at 708 Toulouse Street, is protected by crouching lions on the gateposts. In 1827, the Planter's Bank located there lent money to sugar planters.

## 541 BOURBON (CIRCA 1900), PHANTOM OF THE FRENCH OPERA HOUSE

### *Corner of Toulouse and Bourbon Streets*

The present location of a Four Points Sheridan Hotel was once the site of the French Opera House, designed by James Gallier Jr. and Richard Easterbrook and built in 1859. The rich history of opera in New Orleans dates back to 1796. There were many U.S. premieres at the French Opera, including works by Gounod, Lalo, Rossini and Massenet. It was also home to many carnival balls, receptions and concerts. The billboard advertises, "King Dodo, coming March

"The French Opera House, c. 1900." *Library of Congress.*

20th…a phosphoronic comedy opera." For sixty years, the French Opera was the crown of New Orleans social and cultural life. And, progressively enough, it was a place where slaves and freemen of color were also permitted to see the operas, even if from their own too-lofty fourth tier. The building went into decline and receivership and burned down in 1919—a jewel of Creole architecture, it was a catastrophic loss to the history of the French Quarter. The New Orleans Opera Association continues the tradition. Founded in 1943, it is one of the oldest opera companies in the country.

## 613 ROYAL (1831)

The courtyard (and subsequently the restaurant) got its name, the Court of Two Sisters, from Emma and Bertha Camors, proprietors of a notions store at this location from 1886 to 1906 selling perfumes, lace, gloves, ball gowns—all the accouterments of Creole high fashion. Their clientele gone, the widows closed their shop and

"Old French court yard," 613 Royal Street. This courtyard, with the bronze cupid and fountain, was photographed a few years before Emma and Bertha Camors closed their variety shop in 1906 at 613 Royal Street. It is presently the Court of Two Sisters but without the bronze cupid and fountain. 1903. *Library of Congress.*

moved to a small apartment. In 1944, they died within months of each other in near poverty. The present owners of the restaurant restored the sisters' tomb at St. Louis Cemetery No. 3. The famous bronze cupid at the center of a fountain in the courtyard, maliciously dug up in the early 1930s and sold, is now allegedly decorating the courtyard at the Montegut House at 731 Royal Street.

## 627 ROYAL (CIRCA 1793)

Another structure that escaped the 1794 fire has an easily accessible patio. It is traditionally referred to as "Patti's Court" to honor the

"623 Royal Street, 1937–1938." Jean Baptiste Labatut, attorney general of the Cabildo and aide to Andrew Jackson, originally built a single-story structure in 1795; he later added a second floor and then a third. *Library of Congress.*

brief residency of seventeen-year-old Adelina Patti, the Spanish coloratura soprano who performed a three-month celebrated engagement at the New Orleans French Opera House in 1860.

## 640 ROYAL (1811)

Three of the four levels of "The Skyscraper" building were completed in 1811 by the principal owner and occupant, Dr. Yves LeMonnier, whose monogram is worked into the balcony railing. It was under the ownership of Bertrand Saloy, between 1876 and 1877, that the fourth floor was added, defying the consensus that the entire building would sink.

SIDE STROLL: To the left down St. Peter Street is the so-called Green Shutter House at number 710. Formerly the home of Don Lorenzo Gachet, it is among the oldest surviving structures, built about 1795. The characteristic green shutter color is called "Paris Green" or "arsenical veridian"—it is never monotonous because the sun and rain break it down into shades of green, blue and yellow. Just beyond, at 714 St. Peter, is the Lacoul House (1829), where later, in 1860, master chef Antoine Alciatore from Marseilles opened his first kitchen to serve his borders. Eight years later, on St. Louis Street, he opened Antoine's, which remains one of the most famous restaurants in the country. Number 718 St. Peter, Casa de Flechier, which dates from about 1798, was the home, in 1817, of John Garnier, whose kilns supplied the bricks for many French Quarter homes. It is now the location of famous Pat O'Brien's, which spreads into the exceptional patio area of the structure. It is likely this patio was part of the Tabary Theatre (1820), where grand opera was performed for the first time in the United States. Tradition dictates that after a few of Pat O's Hurricanes, and assuming a resilient stomach, it is essential to eat a Lucky Dog. "Getcha eight inches of fun on a bun" is the pitch of the real-life Ignatius Reillys hawking hot dogs from behind their hot dog–shaped carts. They are always posted on the corner of Bourbon and St. Peter. Next door, at 726 St. Peter, in 1805 was Faisendieu's Tavern, now the home of Preservation Hall. What began in the late 1950s with informal jam sessions has become a world-renowned New Orleans cultural landmark, synonymous with the best of New Orleans traditional jazz. Be certain to line up thirty minutes before the 8:00 p.m. sessions (Preservation Hall information, 504 522 2841).

## 723 ST. PETER, REVEREND ZOMBIE'S VOODOO SHOP

On the way back to Royal Street, cross over to number 723, virtually unchanged since Antoine Angué acquired the building from Antoine Faisendieu in 1809. It is now the location of the fabled Reverend Zombie's Voodoo Shop, one of the two shops (the other is Marie Laveau's House of Voodoo, at 739 Bourbon) that re-create the authentic mysterious ambiance of the old shops in the Quarter that supplied practitioners with their mojo bags, herbs and talismans. Their admixture of tarot card readers; traditional African art; and Brazilian, Cuban and Haitian artifacts captures the early ethnic and spiritual diversity of the French Quarter. Among its most popular spell kits are "Other Attorney Be Stupid" and "Hex Your Ex."

**SIDE STROLL:** Head back to Royal Street, cross, and continue down St. Peter to Number 615 St. Peter (1839). The Arsenal is a three-story Greek Revival building designed by James Daskin. The site was in use since 1728 as a French guardhouse. The Spanish rebuilt it as a prison, which was twice destroyed by fire, in 1768 and again in 1795. It was demolished in 1837, and the present structure was built as the state's defensive

"The Spanish Arsenal, 615 St. Peter St., 1937–1938." *Library of Congress.*

military storage depot. During the Civil War, it was used by Confederate troops to store supplies, and it was the headquarters of General P.G.T. Beauregard until Federal troops captured the city in 1862, at which point it became a military prison. During Reconstruction, it housed the black troops of the Metropolitan Police, who fought with the white anti-integration forces of the Crescent City White League in the Battle for Liberty Place. The league occupied the Arsenal briefly until President Grant dispatched Federal troops to restore order. In 1914, it became part of the Louisiana State Museum complex and exhibits objects of military interest (The Arsenal information, 504-568-6968).

## 632 ST. PETER (1842), DE LASSIZE HOUSE

This house is famous because it's where Tennessee Williams wrote *Streetcar Named Desire* in 1946–47. The Desire trolley line ran down Bourbon Street, to Pauger, then to Dauphine and down to Desire Street in the Bywater District from 1920 to 1948. On its return, it came up Royal to Canal Street. It is anticipated that the Desire line will be restored but running from Rampart down St. Claude to Desire Street. Williams eventually bought 1014 Dumaine Street (1835), where he lived, on and off, until his death in 1983.

## 616 ST. PETER (1790, 1922), LE PETIT THÉÂTRE DU VIEUX CARRÉ

Organized in 1916 as a chapter of the Drama League of America, this is the oldest community theater in the United States. Le Petit has staged musicals and plays since 1922. In 2012–13, it underwent a $1.5 million renovation and now includes Dickie Brennan's Creole

"Le Petit Theatre du Vieux Carre, Chartres and St. Peter Streets." *Library of Congress.*

restaurant, Tableaux. Resist the temptation to go into Jackson Square and return to Royal Street. (Le Petit Théâtre information, 504-522-2081)

*Back to Royal Street*

## 700 ROYAL (1835–40)

Construction of the eleven brick row houses, the "Labranche Buildings," across from "The Skyscraper," was begun by Jean Baptiste Labranche and completed by his widow. The balcony grill, with its intertwined oak leaves and acorns, was part of the original design, but the cascading veils of cast-iron lace from the roof and balcony floors were added in the 1850s, creating one of the most outstanding and memorable sights in the French Quarter.

"700 Royal Street, 1937–1938," the Labranche Building. *Library of Congress.*

## 711 ROYAL STREET (CIRCA 1840)

The twenty-one-year-old Truman Capote, born in New Orleans, returned from New York City and rented a room here in 1925 to pursue his literary career by writing most of his first novel, *Other Voices, Other Rooms*.

## 729–31–33 ROYAL (1795), THE MONTEGUT HOUSE

This is the rather Spanish courtyard of the exceptional Spanish Colonial home constructed for Dr. Joseph Montegut. Born in Armagnac, France, he came to New Orleans in 1769 and served as surgeon major for the Spanish army. Later, Montegut became chief surgeon of Charity Hospital, where he worked without pay. There is a significant painting of his family in the Louisiana State Museum, done by the first identifiable artist in New Orleans, José Francisco

"The Tricou House, 711 Bourbon Street." This particular building, among others
on Bourbon Street, has been the subject of litigation by preservationists and
the anger of its neighbors because successive bar owners have done significant
damage to the historical integrity of the interior and the courtyard. It was built
for Joseph Albert Tricou in 1832, designed by the prominent architects Gurley
and Guillot. The double-hung windows on the second floor reflect growing
American influences on Creole architecture. *Library of Congress.*

"Old French courtyard, Royal Street," c. 1906." *Library of Congress.*

Xavier de Salazar y Mendoza from Merida, Mexico, about 1797. Montegut is buried in St. Louis Cemetery No. 1, tomb 144. It is in this courtyard, presently, that the bronze cupid and fountain, purloined from the Court of Two Sisters, might reside.

## QUADROON BALLS

To the left is Orleans Street, which dead-ends on Royal behind the cathedral. Between Royal and Bourbon Streets, at 717 Orleans, where the Bourbon Orleans Hotel is located, is one of the most likely sites of the most lavish and infamous of the Quadroon Balls held in the early to mid-nineteenth century: the Orleans Ballroom. (The other proposed site is at the Salle de Condé, which was on corner of Madison and Chartres Streets.)

A "quadroon" was a person one-quarter black—the racially mixed mothers of young, light-skinned, elegantly attired quadroon daughters would bring them to these ball events to entertain and dance with wealthy white businessmen, with the hope they would be taken up as mistresses. These arrangements were so-called *mariage de la main gauche*, "left-handed marriages." Many plantation owners kept and supported two families, one on the grounds of the plantation and the other in town, regularly educating their mixed-blood children in France because schooling for blacks was largely illegal in the American South. Marie Laveau, herself the product of a Haitian mixed-blood mother and a white plantation owner, was often asked by the embittered white clients who came to her hair salon to provide them gris-gris to prevent their husbands from per-occupation with their mistresses. To be sure, many young white men went to the balls only to dance, flirt, get drunk or perhaps instigate a duel, and many, many light-skinned women married in the conventional way and raised families with freed black men. The light-skinned children, the *gens de couleur*, or "free people of color," formed an important and vital segment of New Orleans economic and civic life, then and now.

The balls ceased just before the outbreak of the Civil War. The building was acquired by the all-black nuns' order of the Sisters of the Holy Family, founded in New Orleans in 1842 and the oldest female-led African American nuns' order in the United States. It is of special interest that some of the founders of the order were themselves quadroon. The order established St. Mary's Academy, the "first Catholic secondary school for colored girls in New Orleans." In 1962, the sisters left the property, which was becoming dilapidated and a highly coveted piece of real estate, and moved to a new facility at 6905 Chef Menteur Boulevard, where they are presently located. Not without some criticism, the owners of the Bourbon Orleans chose to re-create the antebellum atmosphere at the hotel, evoking a particularly unpleasant memory of New Orleans history.

## SAINT ANTHONY'S SQUARE

Where Orleans Street dead-ends behind the cathedral is St. Anthony's Square, a favorite dueling ground in the 1820s and

1830s. The white obelisk commemorates the men of the French navy's *Tonnerre* who died of yellow fever in 1857. The now-enclosed garden, behind St. Louis Cathedral, is named after the controversial Capuchin monk Padre Antonio de Sedella, who came to New Orleans from Spain in 1781 as an agent provocateur of the Spanish Inquisition. In the liberal religious environment of New Orleans, he was made unwelcome and sent packing back to Spain. He returned in 1783 as Père Antoine, a chastened and humble priest. He became greatly admired for his work among the racially diverse poor, and he served as pastor of the cathedral from 1788 to 1790 and again from 1795 until his death in 1829. It is said that he baptized Marie Laveau and presided at her wedding. He is buried within the cathedral. To the left of the garden, Père Antoine alleyway is named for him. The walkway on the right, Pirate's Alley, honors Jean Lafitte and his crew, and midway down that same alley, at number 624 (1840), is Faulkner House Books. William Spratling, the famous silversmith who later developed the silver industry in Tasco, Mexico, in 1925, sublet the downstairs of this building to William Faulkner, who wrote his first novel, *Soldier's Pay*, here. They later collaborated on *Sherwood Anderson and Other Famous Creoles*, satirizing their bohemian friends living in New Orleans. The bookstore specializes in the work of southern writers and modern first editions. Its annual fundraiser is Juleps in June, it hosts the annual Words and Music Festival and it has revived and published *The Double Dealer*. (Faulkner House Books information, 504-524-2940).

Farther down, the narrow passageway dramatically opens onto the extraordinary expanse of space that is Jackson Square, the pulsing heart of the French Quarter.

# CHAPTER 2
## Jackson Square

Depending on whose government's forces were drilling on the square, it was alternately called Plaza de Armas or Place d'Armes or the Parade Ground; in 1851, it was renamed to honor Andrew Jackson, the hero of the Battle of New Orleans who destroyed General Packingham's invading British troops. Jackson sits on his rearing horse in the exact center of the square, where the flag post stood that flew the colors of Spain, France and the United States. The sculptor Clark Mills's supreme achievement was balancing twenty thousand pounds of bronze without supports. The statue was dedicated on February 9, 1856. Bronze castings of Mills's statue of Jackson are in Washington, D.C., and Nashville, Tennessee. The one here, however, has cut into the granite base: "The Union Must and Shall Be Preserved"—at the insistence of General Benjamin "Beast" Butler, in charge of the occupying Federal troops during the Civil War. There are stone statues of the four seasons in each corner inside the iron fence around the square.

"Jackson Square, c. 1900–1906." *Library of Congress.*

## THE PONTALBA APARTMENTS

Micaëla, the daughter of wealthy Spaniard Don Andrés Almonester y Roxas, was married at the age of sixteen to her twenty-year-old cousin, Joseph Xavier de Pontalba, in an elaborate wedding at the St. Louis Cathedral performed by Père Antoine in 1811. They moved to Paris and, after some years, were divorced, with Micaëla retaining custody of the children and her considerable personal fortune. Joseph Xavier's father apparently thought the family name stained and shot himself in the head after attempting to kill Micaëla. She recovered and returned to New Orleans, immediately undertaking the project of improving the parade ground by enclosing the area with an iron fence, laying out the formal gardens and providing money for the Jackson monument. Micaëla's greatest contribution was commissioning the erection of the Creole-European block-long, red brick, four-story apartments, with sixteen town houses on each side, flanking Jackson Square. She probably came back from Paris with a certain design in mind and dismissed the plans submitted by James Gallier Sr. and those of another architect, Henry Howard. The new contractor, Samuel Stewart, provided most of the floor plans, and the baroness acted as her own architect—making her, in effect, the first female architect in the United States. The work began in 1849 and was completed in 1851. The cast-iron railings bear the baroness's monogram.

The city now owns the buildings on St. Peter (the Upper Pontalbas); the others, on St. Ann Street (the Lower Pontalbas), are owned by the state museum. In the 1920s and '30s, the Upper Pontalba Apartments became the favorites for visiting writers and artists, and the inexpensive apartments were highly coveted. It was the place for literary gatherings that included the likes of Sherwood Anderson, Edna St. Vincent Millay, Thornton Wilder, W. Somerset Maugham, Booth Tarkington and Katherine Ann Porter. Clarence John Laughlin, the father of American surrealist photographers, moved into the fourth-floor attic apartment in the Upper Pontalbas in 1947. Born in Lake Charles, Louisiana, in 1905, when he was a young man, he came to New Orleans with his family. Without much formal education, he nevertheless became a great book collector, especially of art books, which were stacked high on every flat surface in his apartment, including the floor—more than thirty thousand total. At the age of thirty, during the Depression, he taught himself the rudiments of photography and did some work for *Vogue*; however, his greatest body of work was the mysterious and poetical photographs of the decaying buildings in the French Quarter and especially of the ruined plantation homes outside the city. The last group of photographs was published as *Ghosts Along the Mississippi* in 1948. He stopped photographing in the late 1960s and devoted himself to tweaking his images. He held regular soirées at his apartment and lectured widely on his own work. He was a merciless critic of any young photographers who dared show him their portfolios. He sold everything to the Historic New Orleans Collection in 1982 and went to live in Gentilly, a section of New Orleans, with his wife, Elizabeth, until his death in 1985.

## THE SAINT LOUIS CATHEDRAL

The first Catholic church on the site, part warehouse, was destroyed by a hurricane in 1722. The second church, completed in 1727, was destroyed by the great fire of March 21, 1788, which destroyed a considerable number of other structures in the French Quarter The fire began on Chartres Street when a Good Friday devotional candle caught lace curtains on fire. The present structure, known formally as the "Basilica of St. Louis, King of France," was begun in early 1789 and dedicated on December 23, 1794. The expense, about $100,000, was borne by one of New Orleans' greatest benefactors, Don Andrés Almonaster, a native of Andalusia and a knight of the Order of Carlos III. In 1793, Pope Pius VI separated Louisiana from the jurisdiction of the diocese of Cuba, and the first bishop, Don Luis Ignacio María de Peñalver y Cardenas, arrived in 1795. In 1814, the two hexagonal side towers were capped with low spires, and in 1824, the central belfry was added. The clock and its bell came

"Jackson Square and St. Louis Cathedral, c. 1900." *Library of Congress.*

"St. Louis Cathedral, 1937–1938." *Library of Congress.*

from Paris. Perè Antoine, the pastor, baptized the bell "Victory," and it was inscribed in English and French to celebrate Jackson's victory: "Brave Louisianans, this bell whose name is Victory was cast in commemoration of the glorious 8th January 1815."

By 1850, the walls had become weakened, and the architect J.N.B. de Pouilly was commissioned to make the renovations and increase the size to accommodate the new parishioners; however, he and his builder misjudged the strength of the older walls, which collapsed. After extensive reconstruction, the cathedral took its present form, with its three distinctive steeples and façade, and was consecrated in 1851. The cathedral survived all the hurricanes, with occasional repairs, and even a dynamite bomb set off on an afternoon in April 1909 by disputing construction crews. No one was injured in the blast, but the windows and the galleries were damaged. The interior of the cathedral is beautifully decorated with stained-glass windows depicting the life of King Louis IX, the only French monarch elevated to sainthood. The mural in the lunette above the Rococo altar shows King Louis proclaiming the Seventh Crusade to the Holy Land in 1245. The crusade was a failure. In 1250, his army was annihilated in Egypt, and Louis had to be ransomed after four years in captivity. His pious and humble character, his generosity toward the poor and the sick and his devotion to the Catholic Church brought Louis canonization in 1297.

The cathedral is the oldest active Catholic church in the United States, and its two greatest moments were when the rank of "Minor Basilica" was bestowed upon it by Pope John Paul VI in 1964 and when it was visited by Pope John Paul II in 1987.

## THE CABILDO AND THE PRESBYTÈRE

When facing the cathedral, to the left is the Cabildo and to the right is the Presbytère. The Cabildo is separated from the church by Pirate's Alley and the Presbytère, by Père Antoine Alley. Both Spanish-style buildings are brick and stucco with wide porticos and nine semicircular arches supported by Tuscan columns. Almonaster had already hired Gilberto Guillemard to design the cathedral and the Presbytère, and he recommended him for the Cabildo as well—externally, they are virtually identical. The French-style mansard roofs with the dormer windows were added to both buildings in 1847.

At the present site of the Cabildo, the Spanish government, beginning in 1769, twice erected its administrative buildings, which were both destroyed by fires in 1788 and 1794, respectively.

"The Cabildo, c. 1900." *Library of Congress.*

Construction on the present structure, under the guidance of Almonaster, was begun in 1795 and completed in 1799.

The building was named *Casa Capitular*, "Capitol House." The Cabildo was the deliberative body that administered to the municipal affairs during the Spanish domination of the city, replacing the Superior Council, which governed during the French regime. On November 30, 1803, the ceremony retransferring the colony back to France was held within the building, and for twenty days, the building was officially called *Maison de Ville*, "Town Hall." On December 20, 1803, in the *Sala Capitular*, the great auditorium room of the Cabildo's second floor, the colony and the territory were ceded by the French to Generals William C.C. Claiborne and James Wilkinson, representatives of President Thomas Jefferson, in accordance with the Treaty of Purchase of April 30, 1803. The Louisiana Supreme Court met here from 1868 to 1910 and in 1892 ruled on the landmark *Plessy v. Ferguson* case. In 1908, it was dedicated as a historical museum and opened to the public.

The most expensive periods of renovation for the Cabildo, and its sister building the Presbytère, were in the 1930s under the WPA and between 1966 and 1969 by the city and state. After Independence Hall in Philadelphia, the Cabildo is considered the most important historical building in the country. In 1988, a fire in the Cabildo's upper floor caused the roof to collapse. Over a five-year period, the building was restored, as were all the smoke-damaged artifacts and paintings. It was reopened in 1994. The museum's inventory of over one thousand artifacts and works of art are devoted to the history and diverse cultures of Louisiana. On permanent display are one of the three Napoleon death masks and the immense painting by Eugene Louis Lami, completed in 1839, titled *The Battle of New Orleans.*

The site of the Presbytère was the original location of the Capuchin monastery, erected about 1723. In conception, it is of earlier date than the Cabildo and was built entirely by the generosity of Almonaster. Work began in 1792, and the foundations and first floors were finished by 1794. Almonaster's death delayed completion until 1813, when the work was finished by the church wardens. Although intended for ecclesiastical purposes, several municipal courts were located there from 1834 to 1911. The city bought the building and land from the church in 1853, and in 1911, it opened as a division of the Louisiana State Museum. It features exhibits of Mardi Gras artifacts and documents concerning the maritime and cultural history of the city, as well as rotating exhibitions. Along the colonnade is a cannon used in the Battle of New Orleans and what is probably a prototype of *Pioneer*, the Civil War iron submarine, commissioned by the Confederate government to patrol the waters of Lake Ponchartrain and constructed in New Orleans in 1862. It was a three-man vessel, two men pedaling or hand cranking the propeller and one man in the bow with the controls. Its maximum depth was about six feet. (Cabildo and Presbytère information, 504-568-6968)

CHAPTER 3

# The Moon Walk on the Mississippi River

Facing the cathedral, St. Peter Street is on your left. Proceed down that street, under the galleries (balconies are bracketed or self-hanging while galleries are supported by columns) of the Upper Pontalbas and cross Decatur Street. Between Jax Brewery and the street performers' amphitheater is a ramp that leads to the levee. Crossing the streetcar (trolley) and train tracks brings you to the raised Moon Walk promenade named after Maurice "Moon" Landrieu, one of New Orleans' most effective mayors. He is responsible for a project in 1976 making the riverfront once again accessible to pedestrians. To the left is the Governor Nicholls Street Wharfs, which are active shippers' warehouses, and to the right, much farther down, is a music pavilion, the *Natchez* dock and the sixteen acres of Woldenberg Riverfront Park, an ideal place to picnic and listen to roving musicians. Beyond that is the Aquarium of the Americas, which has more than one million gallons of exhibition tanks and, notably, the world's largest collection of jellyfish. Crossing the river are the almost twin spans connecting this side, the East Bank, with Algiers on the West Bank. Algiers is the city's second-oldest neighborhood and is easily reachable with a two-dollar ferry ride from the dock at the foot of Canal Street, just outside the Quarter. There isn't much to do there except stroll among

"Sunday on the levee, c. 1906." Strolling along the river among the cotton bales. *Library of Congress.*

the quaint, picturesque homes in a quiet area largely unperturbed by the twenty-first century—sometimes a welcome relief from the frenetic French Quarter.

## THE RIVER

Abruptly sweeping around the curve of Algiers Point, the river is a boundless source of entertainment and power. The Mississippi is about 2,300 meandering miles in length; from New Orleans upriver to the Gulf is about 125 miles. It's a half a mile wide in front of the city, and its deepest part, about two hundred feet, is at Algiers Point. The average rate of flow at the bend is 3 miles per hour, almost three times the rate anywhere else along the river. The average volume of flow at the bend is 600,000 cubic feet per second—166 semi-trailers of water every second. At the outbreak of the Civil War, New Orleans was the third-largest city after New York and

"High water at New Orleans, La, levee, March 23, 1903." The SS *Proteus* (pictured) was owned by the Southern Pacific Steamship Line of New York City. Starting in 1900, it made runs between New York City and New Orleans. On August 19, 1918, it collided with the oil tanker *Cushing* along the North Carolina coast. One crew member died. Intact, divers frequently explore the ship for its brass-framed stained-glass portholes. *Library of Congress.*

Baltimore and the largest export depot in the world, principally shipping cotton to England and France.

The unloading of bananas was a common sight along the entire wharf area of New Orleans for the first half of the last century; by 1907, New Orleans was the largest importer of bananas in the country. The United Fruit Company was founded in 1899 in Boston, and New Orleans was its principal port in competition with local importers, one of whom, Samuel Zemurray, became president of United in 1933. The company was condemned as exploitative of native workers and of having undue political influence on the Central American areas it dominated economically. Many of the Hondurans who worked on the ships settled in New Orleans and presently represent more than half of the Latino population here.

Today, the Port of South Louisiana is the world's busiest port complex, moving 500 million tons of exported and imported goods

"Unloading bananas from steamer, c. 1900–1910." *Library of Congress.*

"United Fruit Company Banana Conveyer, c. 1910." *Library of Congress.*

"Highwater at New Orleans, La., March 21,1903." The river is at flood stage while cotton bales wait to be loaded on the oceangoing vessels lined up at the dock. *Library of Congress.*

"[Un]loading cotton from the steamship *Warren*" for eventual shipment upriver or to Europe, c. 1880–97. *Photographer W.H. Jackson. Library of Congress.*

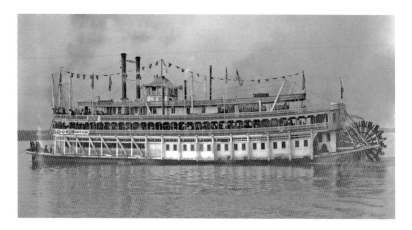

"Steamboat Seeing New Orleans, 1910." *Library of Congress.*

per year. Today, the endless flow of barges and container ships flying the colors of many nations are reminders of the continuing economic importance of New Orleans to the rest of the nation.

Old time riverboats were always at hand—the early steamboats, as they do today, cruised up and down the river to give visitors a view of the city.

The unidentified vessel pictured above is probably the stern wheeler *J.S.*, owned by Acme Packet Co. and capable of carrying 1,500 passengers, brought excursions to New Orleans from St. Louis and farther upriver. It burned soon after this photograph was taken south of La Crosse, Wisconsin. Its banner is dated April 10–15, 1910. "Glad-U-Kum" is a traditional Shriner's welcome. It is likely the steamer was charted by the group since it was holding its Thirty-sixth Annual Session of the Imperial Court that year in New Orleans at the Jerusalem Temple at St. Charles Avenue and Clio Street.

On the river today, the *Creole Queen*, built in 1983 and modeled on the paddle-wheelers of the 1850s, is powered by a diesel electric system and has the capacity to hold one thousand passengers. It is berthed at Canal Street and Riverwalk, near the Hilton, and makes a run to Chalmette, where you can disembark and view the site of the Battle of New Orleans. The iconic *Natchez*, also plying the river, is the ninth boat to bear that name and the only purely steam-driven steamboat built in the twentieth century (1975)—without diesel-electric auxiliary backup. It is modeled on the *Hudson*, which operated from 1886 to 1905, and with engines from the steamboat *Clairton*, which brought coal to New Orleans from 1927 to 1965. It was *Natchez VI*, in 1870, that lost to the *Robert E. Lee* in the famous, and still disputed, race from New Orleans to St. Louis. To comply with Coast Guard regulations, the *Natchez* is built entirely of steel—the only semi-antique elements are the steam engine, the thirty-two-note steam calliope and the copper bell, whose tone was purified by smelting with 250 silver dollars. The *Natchez* makes scenic cruises up and down the river and is berthed at the Toulouse Street Wharf behind Jax Brewery.

As beneficial as the Mississippi has been to New Orleans, aside from the constant dangers of flooding, it also facilitated the spread of disease to the city's population. The rat- and flea-infested dock and the unsanitary conditions aboard ships and within the city itself—stagnant water along the banks, swampy marshes, open sewers and rain cisterns—provided breeding grounds for rats carrying Bubonic plague, cholera from feces-contaminated food and mosquito-borne yellow fever and malaria. The rats were brought under control, but there was no escaping the mosquitoes—the malaria-spreading mosquitoes bite during the night, and those responsible for yellow fever bite during the day. Between 1817 and 1905, it is estimated that forty-one thousand people died of malaria and yellow fever. Ironically, because the city was a virtual laboratory for the growth and spread of disease, it made New Orleans a major center for medical research through LSU's and Tulane's facilities, a reputation sustained since that time.

On the Moon Walk, facing the cathedral directly, a set of stairs permits recrossing the tracks to a short flight of stairs ascending to the elevated plaza of Washington Artillery Park. Here there is an unparalleled view of the full pageantry of Jackson Square on one side, and on the other, the grand Mississippi River. The cannon on site is an 1861 ten-pounder rifled Parrott acquired in 1875. The plaza commemorates the 141st Field Artillery Unit of the Louisiana National Guard, which, some argue, is the oldest military unit in the United States. Its history traces back to about 1725 and, in turn, through its personnel and commanders, to a unit of French-speaking citizens of New Orleans who manned cannon batteries in defense of the city against the invading British. In 1825, the Washington Artillery Unit was selected to fire the cannon salute and to form the honor guard for the Marquis de Lafayette when he visited New Orleans. The unit celebrated its official 100th anniversary in 1939 by firing one round every hour into the Mississippi for one hundred hours. The unit served honorably from the Civil War to the Iraq wars and provided relief to many citizens after Katrina.

Facing the square, to the right, is a down ramp that leads directly to the unmistakable green- and white-striped canopy of the Original Café du Monde Coffee Stand, famous for its beignets, an ancient Acadian pastry fried in Louisiana cotton seed oil and smothered in confectioner's sugar, and its chicory-laced café au lait. New Orleans has always been a coffee-drinking town and one of the chief import docks for raw beans in the country. This landmark café opened in 1862 at its present location, the tip of the old French Market, where the butchers' stalls had been. It is open twenty-four/seven every day except Christmas and during the occasional hurricane. An imaginary tradition permits one, while making a wish, to blow the excess powdered sugar from the beignets on anyone who is at the café for the first time, especially if they are wearing dark clothing. There are seven locations in New Orleans, one in Atlanta and one in Shanghai, China. There are fifty-six locations in Japan (though the Japanese shops miss the point by serving hot dogs along with their beignets).

CHAPTER 4

# Lower Royal Street to Esplanade Avenue

## 523 ST. ANN, 1850 HOUSE

Recross Decatur to St. Ann with Jackson Square on the left and proceed, under the galleries of the Lower Pontalba's, to the corner and Chartres Street. The last row house of the Lower Pontalbas is the 1850 House. In 1948, the Louisiana State Museum re-created an antebellum upper-middle-class merchant's home complete with period furnishings, domestic goods and decorative artifacts reflecting mid-century prosperity. The living quarters are arranged to approximate the residency of widow Amelia Cammack, who lived there with her son, three daughters and from three to seven slaves between 1853 and 1856. One of the chief exhibits is a six-piece bedroom suite crafted by Prudent Mallard originally for Mrs. Magin Puig, who lived at 624 Royal Street. (1850 House information, 504-568 6968)

## 801 CHARTRES (CIRCA 1891)

Across the street on St. Ann, Muriel's Restaurant sits on a plot of land where structures were built virtually from the city's founding in 1718. Some of the most illustrious families—the Destrehans, the Marignys, the Jourdans, the Poydras and the Leveaus—built and rebuilt elegant city homes in this area, places to stay and entertain when they came into town from their plantations. Between 1891 and 1916, Peter Lipari, a wealthy fruit merchant, remodeled number 801 to its present state. Pierre Jourdan owned and lost this residence in a poker game and committed suicide on the second floor. His ghost allegedly manifests as a shimmering light and haunts the building.

## 625 ST. ANN (CIRCA 1725)

This is the location of the first schoolhouse in New Orleans (about 1730?) and presently the Place d'Armes Hotel. The building has a characteristic carriageway with an elegant courtyard and it, too, is haunted—by a bearded headmaster who died along with his family in a fire that destroyed the building. According to some accounts, there is also a twelve-year-old girl, Melissa, seen in a white lace communion dress, who died in another fire in the mid-nineteenth century. She favors Room 508.

With all the fires, yellow fever epidemics, duels, commercial misadventures, gambling and wars, it should not be surprising that there are so many ghost stories in the French Quarter. While there are private homes claiming supernatural presences— benign or slightly mischievous—most of the ghosts appear to prefer lingering in the best-known hotels and inns of the French Quarter. While there are ghost tours available, here is a list, in no particular order, of the properties whose marketing departments are convinced show evidence of paranormal activity and the alleged spectral perpetrators:

BOURBON ORLEANS (717 ORLEANS STREET): nuns, a nineteenth-century distraught suicide, a Confederate soldier and a quadroon ballroom dancer.

CREOLE HOUSE (1013 ST. ANN STREET): a doorknob dismantler.

DAUPHINE HOUSE (1830 DAUPHINE STREET): a Victorian couple (the previous homeowners).

HOTEL VILLA CONVENTO HOTEL (621 URSULINE STREET): small children on the fourth floor and a brothel madam.

LAFITTE GUEST HOUSE (1003 BOURBON STREET): a little girl who died of yellow fever and her grieving mother.

OLIVIER HOUSE (828 TOULOUSE STREET): a Confederate soldier and a woman in an elaborate evening gown.

HOTEL MONTELEONE (214 ROYAL STREET): a dozen former employees and guests.

LE RICHELIEU HOTEL (1234 CHARTRES STREET): executed (moaning) Spanish soldiers.

HOTEL MAISON DE VILLE (727 TOULOUSE STREET): a World War II veteran who prefers country music on the radio.

ANDREW JACKSON (919 ROYAL STREET): five African American orphan schoolchildren who died in a fire and the peripatetic ghost of General Andrew Jackson, who died in Nashville, Tennessee.

DAUPHINE ORLEANS HOTEL (415 DAUPHINE STREET): Confederate soldiers and their ladies of the evening.

OMNI ROYAL ORLEANS (621 ST. LOUIS STREET): an eighteenth-century maid who insists on tucking in your bed.

PROVINCIAL HOTEL (1024 CHARTRES STREET): wounded Confederate soldiers, doctors and nurses.

CORNSTALK HOTEL (915 ROYAL STREET): children laughing and playing.

*For a complete rundown on ghostly New Orleans, see Troy Taylor's Haunted New Orleans (Charleston, SC: The History Press, 2010).*

## 800 ROYAL STREET (CIRCA 1800)

Turning to the right on Royal Street, the Spanish Colonial–style Lanquille Building supports a distinguished wraparound balcony and gallery and contains an elaborate Italianate courtyard. The three-story structure was the first "skyscraper" in the French Quarter. The building was owned by Don Francisco Balthazar and his descendants until 1883.

## 801 ROYAL (CIRCA 1788?)

This building was erected by John Durel as a furniture and linen shop.

## 812–14 ROYAL STREET (1832)

The Lefebre Building was constructed as a commercial venture by Felix Lefebre, a coal, lumber and brick merchant. It has a cast-iron railing motif of grapes and leaves, the most common in the French Quarter.

## 821 ROYAL STREET (1811)

This building was constructed by Jacques César Paillette, born in France, in 1764. He came from an immensely rich and prominent family—his father was a knight of the Legion of Honor. He came to New Orleans from Jamaica with his wife, Angélique Julie Hippolyte Geneviève Durand de Linois. He was a lawyer and had an office on the 200 block of Royal.

## 823 ROYAL (CIRCA 1800)

The owner of the property in 1803 was Daniel Clark, a prominent Irish merchant who was the first representative from Louisiana to the federal Congress. Along with Governor William C.C. Claiborne, Louisiana's first American governor, and the city's mayor, Nicholas Girod, Clark officially welcomed Jackson when he returned from Pensacola to prepare New Orleans' defenses. Later, after a dispute with Governor Claiborne, Clark shot him in the leg in a duel. Alberta Kinsey, who painted many notable French Quarter scenes, had her studio here in the 1930s.

## 824 ROYAL STREET (CIRCA 1805)

This was the residence of Jean Baptiste and has an especially noteworthy iron balcony grill.

## 825–31–33 ROYAL STREET (CIRCA 1790)

This was the town house of John Turnbull, whose principal residence was his plantation in West Feliciana Parish, what was then West Florida. John and his brother Walter arrived from England in the 1770s. In addition to cotton and sugar, the Turnbulls traded fur pelts and horses with the Chickasaw and Choctaw. The family archives indicate that Turnball imported indigo and slaves from Jamaica. It appears his wife, Catherine, owned the property and rented it out. While the interior rear areas are more or less original, the façade has been altered considerably. It is one of the few setback buildings in the French Quarter, providing it with a large courtyard at the front.

## 840–42 ROYAL STREET (CIRCA 1808)

In 1809, this was the home of prominent socialites Thomas Porée and his wife, Loise Foucher, where they lived with their five children. They acquired the building in 1808 for $8,430. They sold it to John Martin in 1818 for $15,000—the equivalent in today's dollars of approximately $272,727. The most recent (2011) asking price was $900,000. For the sake of comparison, the value of $15,000 of gold in 1815 is today approximately $1,200,000.

SIDE STROLL: At the next intersection, Dumaine Street, proceed to the right to 632 Dumaine, Madame John's Legacy, which shares the distinction of being one of the two oldest structures in the Mississippi Valley along with the Ursuline Convent down the street (see 1114 Chartres). The structure represents the simple residential design of the French West Indies, unlike the more ornate Spanish style that would predominate after the fire of 1795. The complex consists of three buildings and an L-shaped courtyard: the main building, with a double-pitched, hipped roof with ventilating dormers, fronting on the banquette (sidewalk); the kitchen and cook's quarters; and the two-story "servants' [slave] quarters." The dwelling space on the second floor sits on a nine-foot stuccoed (plastered) brick storage area that protects from floods and dampness.

It is likely there were structures of some sort on the property since 1722, but the first recorded was erected by sea captain Jean Pascal in 1728. He came to New Orleans with his wife, Elizabeth Real, and their child from France in 1726. He died in the Natchez Indian uprising in 1729. His widow remarried François Marin, a neighbor who had earlier sold Pascal the original lot, at that time extending to Royal Street and almost to Chartres Street. They sold some of the property on each side and built a home much like what is presently there. She operated an inn there until her death in 1777. Her grandson sold the building to a trader, who almost immediately resold it to Renato

"Madam John's Legacy, 1937," 632 Dumaine Street. *Library of Congress.*

Beluch, a wigmaker from France. His son, with the same name as his father and born in the house, became a privateer and a lieutenant of Jean Lafitte's, with whom he fought the British from the battlements at Chalmette. Later, he served as an admiral in the Venezuelan Revolutionary Navy and was a friend of Simón Bolívar.

In 1783, Beluche sold the property to Manuel de Lanzos, a regimental captain in the Spanish colonial military stationed in the Plaza d'Armas. He lived there with his Panamanian wife, Gertrudis Guerrero, six daughters and four slaves. The house suffered severely in the fire of 1788, but de Lanzos, salvaging undamaged elements and with the assistance of Robert Jones, an immigrant American builder, repaired the building within a year. Fortunately, it was one of the few buildings untouched by the deadly conflagration of 1795. From 1823 to 1820, it was owned by Dominique Seghers and his wife, both Belgian immigrants to New Orleans. In 1820, it was purchased by the widow of Jacques Etienne Roman for herself and her two sons, one of whom built Oak Alley Plantation. The other became twice governor of the state. It is likely at this period (1820–36) that the dormers were added and permanent "servants' quarters" built. Between 1847 and 1896, it was owned by Governor Claiborne's son.

In 1879, George Washington Cable, a New Orleans native considered to be the first modern southern writer, published a collection of short stories, *Old Creole Days*, which included "'Tite Poulette." Set at 632 Dumaine, the story is about Zalli, a mixed-blood mistress of Captain John, and their daughter, Petite Poulette. If they had been married, which was against the law, she would have been "Madam John." On his deathbed, he wills the house to her. Misguided, she sells the house, deposits the cash, the bank promptly fails and she loses everything. Thereafter, the house numbered 632 Dumaine was always referred to as "Madam John's Legacy" by all the locals.

As the French Quarter fell into decline near the end of the nineteenth century and filled with immigrants, Madam John's Legacy was acquired, in 1892, by John Baptiste Canepas, an Italian immigrant grocer, probably from Sicily, who eventually opened a real estate company, becoming a substantial property owner in New Orleans. He divided the building into tenement apartments— one on the second floor, three in the servants' quarters and one in the stables. Mrs. Stella Hirsch Lemann acquired it in 1925, and it became something of a bohemian artists and writers' residence. In 1947, she gifted it to the state museum.

A storm in 1952 and Hurricane Betsy in 1965 caused extensive damage to Madam John's, and it became unsafe for habitation. Fortunately, the city's preservationists had formed the Vieux

Carré Commission (1937) and the Vieux Carré Property Owners Association (1938), both organizations mandated to prevent and reverse the general squalor that was overwhelming the French Quarter and to combat "demolition by neglect." The funds were raised for a complete and scrupulous restoration of Madam John's in 1974 using existing material and the original plans. It reopened as part of the state museum system in 1975, and unscathed by Katrina, it continues to display a rotating exhibit of regional art and a permanent collection of artifacts associated with the families who owned the building. (Madam John's Legacy information, 568-6968)

As robust as the numerous owners of Madam John's Legacy were, they apparently would have been no match for Ann Rice's vampire Lestat, who regularly dined on entire French Quarter families and was training little Claudia to do the same. The film *Interview with a Vampire* includes an exterior shot of Madam John's showing numerous coffins of family members being removed from the building and hoisted onto a horse-drawn hearse.

*Back to Royal Street*

## 900–06–10 Royal (1838),
### the Mildenberger Buildings

Dr. Christian Mildenberger and his wife, Marie Aimée Mersier, coming to New Orleans via Cuba, were likely among the many refugee plantation owners who fled the successful 1791 slave uprising in Santo Domingo (Haiti). He served as the surgeon under Major Plauche at the Battle of New Orleans and was instrumental in the corrected treatment of yellow fever—the "Black Vomit" epidemics— not only in New Orleans, but also in New York and Philadelphia, by theorizing the disease was not contagious. Developing one of the largest sugar plantations, Mildenberger became one of the wealthiest men in New Orleans. Some years after his death in 1829, his wife commissioned the three connected row houses, one each for their sons, Aristide, Gustave and Joseph Alphonse. The latter's daughter, Alice Heine, prophetically born on Royal Street, became the toast of Paris at the age of seventeen and married the seventh Duke of Richelieu, Marquis de Jumulhac, in 1875. Upon his death five years later, he left Alice seventeen million francs. In 1889, she married Albert I, prince of Monaco.

## 915 ROYAL (CIRCA 1850)

Sometime after the original building on this property, owned by the first chief justice of Louisiana, was destroyed by fire, it was replaced by the present Victorian-style mansion, now the Corn Stalk Hotel. The original owner of the mansion, Dr. Joseph Biamenti, commissioned the famous fence, erected in 1859, from Wood & Perot, the illustrious iron foundry in Philadelphia. His wife, allegedly, was yearning for the cornfields of her childhood. It is possible, however, that the fence and its unpainted twin uptown at 1148 Fourth Street were cast by the foundry's subsidiary in New Orleans. To the stalks of corn and the intertwined pumpkin vines on the posts, the gate design adds a butterfly and a sprig of holly.

## 916–24 ROYAL (1838)

This was the home of Joachim Kohn, an immigrant from Bohemia who was an attorney and director of the New Orleans Canal and Banking Company. He and his wife, Marie, had three children: Samuel, Joseph and Marie Amelie Kohn. He died in Paris in 1866. His portrait by Jean-Joseph Vandechamp hangs in the state museum.

## 919 ROYAL (CIRCA 1889)

On this site, a Spanish schoolhouse, built in 1792, was destroyed in a fire. Between 1812 and 1823, a new structure served as the Federal District Court where Jackson was brought to trial in 1815 for allegedly superseding his authority in maintaining martial law in the city. When he refused to answer the court's questions, he was found in contempt; however, at the insistence of the Louisiana legislature, the thousand-dollar fine levied against Jackson was returned with interest in 1844, the year before his death.

## 934 ROYAL (CIRCA 1830S, WITH RENOVATIONS CIRCA 1850), THE BEAUREGARD HOUSE

P.G.T. Beauregard, the first brigadier general of the Confederacy, was born twenty miles outside New Orleans in St. Bernard Parish. He was the South's best tactician, but although successful at Fort Sumter, the First Battle of Bull Run and the Second Battle of Petersburg, he was at constant loggerheads with other generals and especially with Jefferson Davis, the president of the Confederacy. When the Civil War was over, he was offered commands in the armies of Egypt, Romania and Brazil. He chose instead to return to New Orleans and, from 1865 to 1876, served as head of a small railroad line and railway company. Beauregard participated actively in the political life of the city and was an outspoken proponent of the civil and voting rights of freed slaves. He achieved significant wealth when, with Jubal Early, another Confederate general, he was spokesman for fifteen years of the Louisiana lottery. Despite his best efforts at reform, the lottery was completely corrupt, and Beauregard's reputation was somewhat tarnished by his association.

Beauregard rented this home, his primary residence in the French Quarter, from 1868 to 1875 and lived there with his son René. He is buried in the Tomb of the Army of Tennessee in Metarie Cemetery in New Orleans. There is a bronze equestrian of Beauregard at the circle where Esplanade runs into the New Orleans Museum of Art. The statue was created (in 1915) by Alexander Doyles, who earlier executed the statue of Robert E. Lee (in 1884) uptown at Lee Circle.

SIDE STROLL: Take a left on St. Philip to Bourbon Street, where you'll find Lafitte's Blacksmith Shop Bar, 941 Bourbon Street (circa 1772). To the left and down a residential block to Bourbon Street is Lafitte's Blacksmith Shop, a classic example of French Colonial town house architecture with its characteristic hip roof and "briquette en entre poteaux" (soft brick wedged between cypress beams). There is another example at 901 Burgundy, but it was reconstructed from a home moved to the French Quarter from River Road in 1770 by Gabriel Peyroux.

There is attached to Lafitte's Blacksmith Shop imperishable folklore; however, not only does its meager fireplace preclude it from ever having been used by a blacksmith, but also Jean and Pierre Lafitte never built it, never rented it, never used it

"Lafitte's [Blacksmith] Cottage, 941 Bourbon, 1937–1938." *Library of Congress.*

as an emporium for stolen swag and probably never set foot in it, at least according to the notarial records extending back to 1722. At that time, it belonged to Jean Cossine, who then sold it to Nicolas Touze. In 1771, it was owned by Pedro Revoil. Either he or Bartholome Robert, the next owner (1772), built the structure. It is at this time (1772–91) that tradition holds it was owned or at least used by the brothers Lafitte; however, the property remained in the hands of the Robert family and, through marriage, the Durocher family until 1833. Nowhere in the history of either family is there a suggestion they hobnobbed with pirates. There were many subsequent owners living there until the 1950s, when it became Café Lafitte Bar, perhaps the first gay bar in the United States. New management, however, caused employees and patrons to open Café Lafitte in Exile up the street at 901 Bourbon.

Having survived the fires of 1788 and 1794, urban blight at the turn of the twentieth century and the commercialism of the twenty-first century, it remains an affectionate and timeless memorial to a man idolized by the citizens of New Orleans. What not to admire, after all, about a man who, when Governor Claiborne offered $500 for his capture, waggishly reciprocated by offering three times (some say thirty times that amount for the governor's capture (some say for his head) and deliverance to his stronghold on Grand Isle in Barataria Bay. And later, ungrudging, he supplied the rifle flints, gunpowder and cannoneers without which Jackson could not have prevailed against the British (for which patriotic deed President Madison officially forgave Lafitte his piratical sins). Lafitte, however, was Lafitte, and bored by city life, he gathered up his Baratarians, went back to his old ways and disappeared into legend—although many patrons, especially after a few whiskey sours or sazeracs, make out his ghostly form, tweaking his mustache, hovering in the rafters of the old building.

*Back to Royal and left*

## 1000 BLOCK OF ROYAL STREET

The flag flying from the gallery in the photo below indicates that the homeowner was either a former king of Rex or a member of the Mardi Gras Carnival Association (krewe) formed, in part, to celebrate the visit to New Orleans of the Grand Duke Alexandrovitch Romanoff of the Russian Empire in 1872. The colors of the banner—purple and green with a gold band in between—became the official colors of Carnival. The trolley, marked "Clio," is heading toward Canal Street, and its destination is a few blocks past Lee Circle.

The 1000 block of Royal Street has its share of French Quarter history. Number 1027 Royal (circa 1800?), for example, was owned by Patrick MacNamara, who married Marguerite

"Royal Street, 1000–1100 block, 1890–1901." *Library of Congress.*

Judith Chauvin de Léry des Islets, the daughter of a patrician Creole family. He thereafter preferred to be addressed as "Count" MacNamara. Number 1026–30 Royal (circa 1790) was built by Captain Enrique Mentzinger, a staff officer in the Spanish military. However, the 1000 block has a special place in French Quarter lore, not, in this case, because of famous historical residents, but for fictional ones created by George Washington Cable.

Cable's short story "Clarisse Délicieuse" was published in *Scribner's* in 1875. The story is set in 1830, and all the activity in the story occurs on this street. It was a time when the force of migration of "Americans" into the Creole social and economic structure and customs of New Orleans was being felt. Neither side understood the other. The Yankees seemed brash and too serious to the Creoles, and the Creoles appeared too refined and mildly decadent to the Yankees. It is no surprise that the area in the middle of Canal Street that separated the Creole French Quarter from the Yankee business interests on the other side was then, and forever after, called the "neutral ground." Cable's story is about the ascendancy of "Yankee ideas" and "Yankee notions" and the slow decline of the old aristocratic Creole families. But setting that theme aside, it is Cable's rich depictions of his characters and imaginative use of the 1000 block of Royal and the buildings that imbue this street with a special magic.

Consider the description of young Dr. Mossy's medical office at 1026 Royal, where he aspires to the seriousness of the Yankees:

> *The little one-story, yellow-washed tenement…with its two glass doors protected by batten shutters, and its low, weed-grown tile roof sloping out over the sidewalk…to be frank, the doctor's office was dusty and disorderly—very. It was curious to see jars, and jars, and jars. In them were serpents and hideous fishes and precious specimens of all sorts.*

Across the street, at 1027 Royal, is the "red-brick-front mansion" of the shrewd Madame Clarisse Délicieuse:

> [W]*ith nightfall, its drawing-rooms always sent forth a luxurious light from the lace-curtained windows of the second-story balconies…It was one of the sights of Rue Royale to see its tall, narrow outline reaching high up toward the stars, with all its windows aglow.*

Everyone is waiting for the military parade commemorating the fifteenth anniversary of the Battle of New Orleans to come down the street, at the head of which is Dr. Mossy's estranged father, General Hercule Mossy de Villivicencio, a representative of the old order—a little vain, a little uncomprehending of the Creoles' loss of power:

> *The houses of Rue Royale gave a start and rattled their windows…and now there comes a distant strain of trumpets, and by and by the drums and bayonets and clattering hoofs, and plumes and dancing banners; far down the street stretch out the shinning ranks of gallant men…In the front, towering above his captains, rides General Villivicencio, veteran of 1814–15, and with the gracious pomp of the old-time gentleman, lifts his cocked hat, and bows, and bows.*

The marchers are greeted by the young ladies on the balcony of Madame Clarisse:

> *Of the two balconies which overhung the banquette on the front of the Délicieuse house, one was a small affair, and the other deeper and broader one, from which Madame and her ladies were wont upon gala days to wave handkerchiefs and cast flowers to the friends in the procession…It was a bright blue day, and the group that quite filled the balcony had laid wrappings aside, as all flower-buds are apt to do on such Creole January days, and shone resplendent in spring attire…Madame Délicieuse's balcony was a perfect maze of waving kerchiefs.*

SIDE STROLL: Walk down Royal Street to the next intersection, Ursuline Street, and take a right down to the next street, Chartres. Take an immediate left to 1113 Chartres, the Beauregard-Keyes House (1826–1827). This famed and dramatic building, with its Ionic and Tuscan colonnades, was designed for Joseph le Carpentier by François Correjolles from St. Domingue (Haiti). His daughter, Louise Thérèse, lived there with her husband, Alonso Murphy—it was here that master chess prodigy Paul Morphy was born. Novelist Francis Parkinson Keyes rented the building as her winter residence (she spent the summers in New Hampshire) from 1944 until her death in 1970.

In 1833, Carpentier sold the house to John Merle, the Swiss consul, who established the formal parterre gardens. He sold the house to the widow of Colonel Manuel Andry, a planter from St. Charles Parish. The next owner was Dominique Lanata from Genoa, the consul from Sardinia, who then sold it to Pietro Giacona and his son, Corrado, in 1904. The Giaconas were in the "wholesale" liquor business—which is to say, they either sold liquor without federal tax stamps or they had their own

"Chartres Street, Vieux Carre." The Beauregard-Keyes House, 1113 Chartres Street, c. 1900–06. *Library of Congress.*

distillery. In 1909, the Giaconas were attacked by members of a rival Mafia syndicate while they were sitting on the gallery, either in revenge for the shooting of the brother-in-law of one of the attackers or because the Giaconas refused to pay for "protection." The story is confused, but either the Giaconas shot and killed three of the four attackers in the street or in the back of the house or, as another version has it, they escaped the attack and later invited the men over for a sit-down, during which Pietro and Corrado shot three of the four at dinner.

Sicilian organized crime groups like the Black Hand were established in New Orleans before the Civil War, and by the 1880s and 1890s, as the French Quarter began to deteriorate and provide cheap tenement dwellings for immigrant workers, the lower Quarter was the scene of considerable violence as rival factions fought for dominance on the docks, bootlegging and extortion. It culminated in 1890 with the assassination of Chief of Police David Hennessey and the subsequent mob execution of eleven imprisoned Italians, all of whom had been found innocent and were to be released from custody. Corrado Giacona became the dominant boss of the Mafia in New Orleans from 1922 to 1944. For the most part, the mob in New Orleans operated independently of New York City and Chicago and was often at odds with their dictates.

By the 1920s, the Beauregard-Keyes House, as did the rest of the lower French Quarter. fell into disrepair and neglect. It was saved from demolition and conversion to a macaroni factory by a civic-minded citizens' group. They put some of Beauregard's personal effects on display in the front rooms and opened it up to the public; however, it was not until Keyes began to renovate in earnest that the house was brought back to its full grandeur. During her residency, she wrote many historical Louisiana-related novels and two imaginative biographies of previous inhabitants: Paul Morphy (*The Chess Players*, 1960) and Beauregard (*Madam Castel's Lodger*, 1962). She also wrote her most famous novel here, the murder mystery

*Dinner at Antoine's* in 1948. Many of her manuscripts are on view in the house along with her famous doll collection and her porcelain *veilleuses* (teapots heated by candles). In the 1960s, the Garden Study Club of New Orleans used the original plans to restore the gardens, providing blooming flowers year round. (Beauregard-Keyes House information, (504 523-7257)

## 1114 CHARTRES STREET (1745–52), OLD URSULINE CONVENT

The cornerstone for the first convent, designed by Michael Zeringue, was set in 1730, and the building was completed in 1734. Unfortunately, the brick between-posts were not protected by plaster or stucco, and within twelve years considerable deterioration set in and some of the walls became unsettled. Near the site, a new structure of stucco-covered brick, designed by Ignace François Broutin and built by Claude DuBreuil, was erected (in 1749–53) using salvage from the former structure—most significantly, the winding cypress staircase. The convent was declared a National Historic Landmark in 1960, and it was noted, "This is the best surviving example of French colonial public architecture in the country." The structure underwent considerable restoration between 1973 and 1978. The convent and Madame John's Legacy are the two oldest structures in the Mississippi Valley.

The Ursuline nuns arrived in New Orleans in 1727, sailing for five months from Rouen, France, under the protection of Louis XV to minster to the settlers. By the best accounting, there were eight nuns, one novice and two candidates. In their temporary quarters in what is now the Lower Garden District, their first responsibility was to look after a group of newly arrived women, *Filles à la Cassette* ("Casket Girls"). These were women, along with a dowry chest, sent to the French colonies by the king to encourage the growth of families. All these young ladies were in the charge of the Ursulines, who chaperoned them until they were chosen for marriage. The arrival of these young ladies very likely occurred, although there

"The Archbishopric, 1890–1901." The convent and St. Mary's Church. *Library of Congress.*

seems to be no documentary evidence in the Ursuline archives. Louis XIV certainly did send the *Filles du Roi* ("Daughters of the King") to the French Canadian colonies earlier, in 1663–73, to encourage community growth. Nevertheless, because the dowry chests are referred to as "caskets," the term as been often mistranslated back to French as *Filles à la Casquette*, which is actually French for "Daughters of the Cap." However, this has allowed those infatuated with Anne Rice to suggest that the young ladies were actually transporting vampires in caskets from the Old World to New Orleans.

After the long delay, the Ursulines moved into the new structure in late 1753. They provided the first professional medical care, and part of the convent served as a hospital during yellow fever outbreaks. They planted an extensive herb garden, and Sister Francis Xavier became, in effect, the first female pharmacist in the New World, researching, cataloging and prescribing certain herbs for various maladies. Their principal role, however, was to work among the poor and to educate not only the elite daughters of the colonists (among them the future Baroness de Pontalba) but additionally, although in separate quarters, free women of color, female slaves, Native American women and orphan girls. They occupied the building to 1824, until they felt their privacy infringed on when city officials decided to extend Chartres and Governor Nichols Streets through the convent's property. The nuns turned the building and property over to the city's bishop, moved two miles out of the city and rebuilt the convent a third time.

In 1831, the state legislature rented the building for several sessions when its offices burned down, and later, the building briefly became the state capitol. When the lease was up, the nuns donated the property to the archbishop for his residence and for his successors. In addition to being a museum of religious artifacts, paintings of prominent prelates and special exhibitions, it is now a research facility for Archdiocesan archival material and is where important ecclesiastical documents are signed. In the garden, statues commemorate the founding Ursuline nuns, Saint Frances Xavier Cabrini and Father Francis Xavier Seelos.

The third convent also ran up against an expanding city and was demolished in 1912 to make room for the Inner Harbor Navigation Canal linking the Mississippi to Lake Pontchartrain. The Ursulines moved again, this time founding the Ursuline Academy on St. Charles Avenue, the oldest continually operating Catholic school and the oldest girls' school in America.

The Ursuline Convent is the official residence of the archbishop of the Roman Catholic Archdiocese of New Orleans. The city was elevated to the rank of diocese in 1793 by Pope Pius VI. The patron saints of the archdiocese are Our Lady of Prompt Succor and Saint Louis, king of France. (Old Ursuline Convent information, 504 529-3040)

## 1116 CHARTRES STREET (1845), SAINT MARY'S ITALIAN CHURCH

This exquisite church adjacent to the Ursuline Convent was used as a chapel for the archbishop. It has a superb Baroque-style sanctuary,

"1133–1135 Chartres St." Soniat-Dufossat House, 1937–38. *Library of Congress.*

an elaborately carved marble altar, ornamented railings and steps and a beautiful series of stained-glass windows. In the choir loft is the organ made by the esteemed Pilcher Bros. of New Orleans, rescued and restored from the convent's demolition site. Above the monumental doors, the frieze depicts two angels in flight holding a chalice. Above that it is the Latin: "This is the House of God and the Gate to Heaven." And just above the elegant rose window and below the papal coat of arms, the Latin reads: "Dedicated to the Virgin Mother of God."

The church has had several names. Originally, it was called Sante Marie de l'Archevêché during the tenure of Bishop Antoine Blanc, and later, in 1921, it became St. Mary's Italian Church, with the masses in Italian to serve the local parishioners. In 1976, it was rededicated as Our Lady of Victory, to commemorate the nuns' prayer vigil on behalf of Jackson and his troops. In 1994, prominent Italian citizens convinced Archbishop Francis Shulte to restore the name to St. Mary's Italian Church, which is now the church's official designation.

## 1133 CHARTRES (1829, 1834), SONIAT-DUFOSSAT HOUSE

The construction of the first two of the town houses in this complex (now the Soniat House Hotel) is attributed to François Boisdoré, a freeman of color, for Tchoupitoulas Plantation owner Joseph Soniat du Fossat. A few years later, his son built the third contiguous house. The baronial French family is descended from Chevalier Guy Soniat du Fossat, who came to Louisiana in 1751 and wrote one of the earliest histories of the city, from its founding to 1791.

A member of the family, Edmond, sold an investment property at 1140 Royal to Mme. Delphine Macarty LaLaurie in 1831, inadvertently precipitating the most notorious legend in the French Quarter: the Haunted House.

*Head to the left down Governor Nicholls Street and cross Royal Street*

## 718 GOVERNOR NICHOLLS, SPANISH STABLES

This complex of buildings is collectively, and sometimes individually, referred to as the "Spanish Stables," although the Spanish were

"718 [716–24, the courtyard] Gov. Nicholls, 1937–1938." *Library of Congress.*

long gone when these buildings were constructed and redesigned between 1809 and 1835. In the 1960s, they were renovated into apartments by Clay Shaw. Shaw was arrested on March 1, 1967, by New Orleans DA Jim Garrison and charged with complicity in a plot to assassinate JFK. Shaw was completely exonerated. A plaque in front of the building honors Shaw's contribution to preserving the history of the French Quarter.

*Back to Royal Street*

## 1140 ROYAL STREET (CIRCA 1830), HAUNTED HOUSE

Delphine and her third husband, Dr. Louis LaLaurie, furnished their new home here with exquisite European trappings, and they moved easily among the Creole aristocracy. However, rumors began to spread that have proven unquenchable for almost two hundred years. The following report is from an account written by Marie L. Puents in the *Daily Picayune* on March 13, 1892:

"The Haunted House, c. 1900–1906." *Library of Congress.*

"1140 Royal Street, 1937–1938," the Haunted House. *Library of Congress.*

*Her manners were sweet, gracious and captivating, her voice was said to be as soft as a low strain of music; even in New Orleans she was noted for her charitable deeds, and yet—and yet—there were wild rumors that madame inflicted the most cruel fortune upon her slaves, that she whipped and flogged them unmercifully, that in that splendid house behind those attic windows were human beings chained to the floor, confined to dankness and actually starving to death.*

Certain neighbors claimed to hear cries of distress coming from the house, and in 1833, one claimed to have seen a black child throw herself off the roof to her death trying to evade her mistress's whip. All of these accounts were exacerbated by *The New Orleans Bee* on April 11, 1834, a local paper that reported on a fire in the kitchen deliberately started by a servant chained to the stove. When a crowd collected to assist in saving the contents of the house, they found slaves deformed by their iron collars and chains and half-dead behind a locked door. There were always severe penalties for the abuse of slaves in New Orleans, and the next night an even larger crowd, filled with indignation, stormed and almost destroyed the house, pitching the furniture and china onto the street. Madame LaLaurie (and her husband in some versions) evaded the crowd and escaped in her carriage to Bayou Saint John, where she got a small boat to take her across Lake Ponchartrain to Mandeville, from whence, allegedly, she made her way to Mobile and then to Paris. According to some accounts, she lived happily and died in Paris and was buried there. George Washington Cable, in *Strange True Tales of Louisiana* (1888), claims she was killed, gored by a wild boar on a hunt outside Paris. Others claim she never left New Orleans or that her body was secretly returned and buried in New Orleans.

Over the decades, the plight of the slaves was made more lurid. Delphine became a sadistic monster, and dozens of psychics and ghost hunters have "detected" around the exterior of the house continual paranormal activity of all the unquiet spirits of the maimed and tortured slaves. It was pointed out in 1934 that the neighbor responsible for spreading the rumors about the LaLaurie household was incensed that Delphine had been appointed administrator of that neighbor's brother's estate and that she had every malicious reason to spread rumors in order to ruin Delphine's name, but this information has not restored any part of Delphine's reputation—well, perhaps a little. A book called *Mad Madame LaLaurie: New Orleans' Most Famous Murderess Revealed* (Charleston, SC: The History Press, 2011) suggests it was her husband who was guilty of performing medical experiments on their servants; however, Madame LaLaurie's infamy is sealed in wax at the Musée Conti Wax Museum, where she is depicted overseeing the whipping of a slave in her attic. The building's legends accumulated through the decades. It was sold several times, but tenants never stayed—too many windows and doors mysteriously opening and closing.

After the Civil War, during Reconstruction, it was turned into a school for both black and white girls. But by 1878, as segregation took hold, it became briefly a black high school. In 1882, it became, again briefly, a music conservatory, but the director's reputation was destroyed by slander (like Delphine's?). During the New Orleans World Industrial and Cotton Centennial Exposition in 1884–58, it became a short-lived boardinghouse. The next owner (1889–92) was an eccentric antiques dealer, Jules Eppard Vigne, who was so reclusive that it was days before neighbors found him in the attic dead on an iron cot. The neighbors also found about $10,000 stashed in some of his pillows. In 1923, the building was sold to William Warrington, who established a residence for homeless men. From 1932 to 1942, it was owned by the Scottish Rite Masons. For a long while, it was owned by a doctor who lived in the front of the house and rented out five apartments.

If there ever was a curse on the building, however, it came down hard on Nicholas Cage, the last private owner of the building. In 2007, he bought the building for $3.45 million; he lost it to a foreclosure, and the bank acquired it for $2.3 million in 2011. Cage's New Orleans real estate "investments" extend to St. Louis Cemetery No. 1, where he has acquired a plot. That area of the cemetery is referred to as, in good humor, "Nicholas Cage Plaza." He has erected a nine-foot pyramid for his future entombment—unless, of course, the bank forecloses.

Earlier in 2007, Angelina Jolie and Brad Pitt bought 521 Governor Nichols (circa 1830), just two blocks away, for $3.5 million. Although it was widely reported in January 2010 that Angelina regularly told Brad, "I hate New Orleans," she seems to have settled into French Quarter life, and they visit often. More importantly, it has allowed Pitt, a devoted lover of New Orleans and an environmentalist, to continue the work of his Make It Right Foundation, developing at least 150 eco-friendly homes in the Katrina-devastated Lower Ninth Ward. All the homes, designed by some of the world's best-known architects, moderately subsidized, were open first to returning residents of the area and are now open to first responders and teachers as well. The foundation has been criticized for not adhering to the traditional housing types in the area; however, Brad Pitt has helped create a significant contribution to the architectural history of New Orleans. The homes are about twenty minutes by cab, just over the North Claiborne Bridge (United Cab Co., 504 522-9771).

*From 1140 Royal Street, walk back up half a block to 1132 Royal Street*

## 1132 ROYAL STREET (1857–60, 1971), GALLIER HOUSE MUSEUM

On a plot of land once part of the Ursuline nuns' land grant, James Gallier Jr. designed and built this Greek Revival home as his personal residence, where he lived with his wife, Agalé Villavaso, and their four daughters. His father, born in Ireland in 1798 (the family name was Gallager), came to New Orleans via New York City in 1833. Between them, the Galliers designed some of the most important public and private buildings in the city. When Gallier Sr. turned over his architectural business to his son, he and his wife traveled widely. In 1866, Gallier drowned when the *Evening Star* capsized off the coast of North Carolina. Tragically, his son died two years later, at the age of forty-one, possibly of yellow fever, but Gallier's innovative design genius lives on in Gallier House.

Descendants of the family lived in the building until 1917, and it thereafter fell into disrepair. However, in 1965, Sandra and Richard Freeman, with the Ella West Freeman Foundation, acquired the building and began a meticulous restoration of the exterior and interior to reflect the lifestyle of an upper-class Creole family in the 1860s. The work was completed in 1971, and it was soon opened to visitors. The care exercised in correctly representing the house year round is reflected in the fact that as the summer months approach— the ritual is called "Summer Dress"—all the upholstered furnishings are covered in white canvas slipcovers, the woolen carpets and rugs are replaced with sisal mats and all the heavy drapes used to ward

"1140 Gallier House," 1132 Royal Street, 1937–1938. *Library of Congress.*

off the cold are replaced by sheer curtains. There is a telling contrast between all the opulent furnishings of the Gallier household and the starkness of the servants' quarters. Tulane University was custodian of the building from 1986 until it passed into the stewardship of the Women's Exchange in 1996. (Gallier House information, 504 525-5661)

## 1101–41 ROYAL STREET (1831–32), "STREET OF BALCONIES"

All the buildings across from Gallier House were built at the same time by La Compagine des Architects and sold individually at auction. Somewhat later, all the galleries were widened and extended to the street, giving them a distinctive appearance.

*Head back down Royal Street, crossing Governor Nichols Street (1200 block)*
*and Barracks Street (1300 block), down toward Esplanade Avenue*

Worth noting is how more common "American" influences are present along these blocks—especially in the wood-frame houses set in from the street with "front yards" and the American Victorian gingerbread at 1224–26 (circa 1881).

## 1271 ROYAL STREET (1831), BOULIGNY HOUSE

Charles Dominique Joseph Bouligny was born in New Orleans in 1773. He was the son of Don Francisco Bouligny and Marie Louise Le Sénéchal D'Auberville. He served as a lieutenant in the Louisiana Infantry Regiment, of which his father was brevet lieutenant colonel, and he commanded a gunboat in the Mississippi Squadron. In 1800, he became a member of the Cabildo, serving as *regidor perpétuo* (councilor for life). Although he operated a rum (tafia) producing sugar plantation, he was heavily engaged in the political life of the city, serving as commissioner of the municipal council, justice of the peace and on the Committee for the Defense of the City (1814–15). He was elected to the first Louisiana Territory House of Representatives and served as a major in the territorial militia. He also served in the United States Senate from 1824 to 1829. He and his wife, Anne Arthémise LeBlanc, had thirteen children. The official *Biographical Directory of the United States Congress* states—and it is everywhere repeated—that "he was educated by private tutors." However, because Bouligny was a man of such distinction who served at a critical time in the history of the city, it is important to note that Grace King, who in 1921 published a revered history of the *Creole Families of New Orleans*, wrote, "It was always mentioned of him, and it was a distinction of the time, that he was educated in the public schools of the city."

The 1200 and 1300 blocks of Royal Street on the Sunday before Labor Day traditionally become the gathering place for the Southern Decadence drag queen parade through the French Quarter. Although predominately a gay male event, it attracts the GLBT communities from all over the world—as many as 100,000 have attended—the rallying point being the Golden Lantern Bar at 1239 Royal Street. The parade route varies from year to year.

# CHAPTER 5

# Esplanade Avenue to the U. S. Mint and the French Market

What was originally a portage, a three-mile "path over which canoes and supplies were carried" between the river and Bayou St. John to gain access to Lake Ponchartrain, Esplanade Avenue became the downtown border of the French Quarter running from the Mississippi River to Bayou St. John, the statue of General Beauregard, the New Orleans Museum of Art and the entrance to City Park. Because it is naturally occurring high ground, two to four feet above sea level, it is often called the Esplanade Ridge. In 1822, the city's surveyor, Joseph Pile, referred to it as the "Esplanade Prolongment," and it was this area, an "extension cleared of brush and trees," that the city began to claim, by purchase and litigation, to build a proper avenue to rival the boulevards of Europe. By the 1850s, it was an elegant promenade where many of the wealthy Creole families retreated, concerned about the "American" encroachments into the French Quarter. Others soon came to avoid the hectic noise of commerce along the river. And in the course of one hundred years of development, Esplanade Avenue is a catalogue of exceptional architectural styles in wood and brick: grand mansions, stately town houses, double-galleried homes and cottages.

Less appropriate city planning in the 1960s allowed an I-10 overpass to sever Esplanade, destroy many African American

"Esplanade Avenue, 1900." *Library of Congress.*

business and spread decay on all sides. It is certain now, however, that this will be reversed by the city's Master Plan and with direction from organizations like the Congress of New Urbanism.

## THE CORNER OF ROYAL STREET AND ESPLANADE AVENUE

Before turning the corner to the right (toward the U.S. Mint), note the extensive 704 Esplanade complex on the left corner. The square masonry building fronting on the avenue consists of an attached slave quarters and back house. It was built by John Gauche, a crockery manufacturer, about 1856. It was renovated in 1937 and restored in 1969. The cast-iron railing design is unique. Turn to the right onto the 600 block of Esplanade Avenue and proceed toward the U.S. Mint.

## 640 ESPLANADE (1815)

This hip-roofed masonry, four-room Creole cottage is among the oldest surviving buildings on the avenue. From 1914 through the 1960s, it was the home of a tailor and his business.

## 634–632 ESPLANADE (1885–86), ZAERINGE-BEGUÉ HOUSE

Both buildings, in the Second Empire style, had separate builders and owners but are almost identical, except for the entrances, and the balcony of 634 is canopied.

## 628 ESPLANADE (1868), VILAVASO-MASPERO HOUSE

Although many of the details have been lost, this building is still recognizably in the American late Classical style. Late in the nineteenth century, it was owned by the Maspero family, who, earlier in the century, were prominent slave auctioneers.

## 606–04–02 ESPLANADE (1834)

By 1811, most of these lots were owned by Barbé Desdunes, a free woman of color. The lots were consolidated in 1815, and in 1834, the three buildings with common walls were erected by attorney Henry Raphael Denis. The wraparound cast-iron galleries and railings were added in the 1850s. Number 604 has the distinction of having been owned, if briefly, by Paul Morphy's father, Judge Alonzo Morphy, in 1835. Morphy served as congressman, state attorney general and Supreme Court justice for Louisiana. The judge died in 1856 in a strange way: He was turning to talk to someone behind him and got a cut above his eye from the edge of the man's Panama Hat brim. It resulted in congestion of the brain and death. In the same building, in 1860, Madam Egerie established a "university" to educate young women through the sixth grade.

*Cross Chartres Street to the 500 block of Esplanade*

## 544 ESPLANADE (CIRCA 1860), TIBLIER-CAZENAVE-LANOIS HOUSE

The original buildings on this lot were owned by Marie Beaudequin, a free woman of color. Subsequently, two town houses with a common wall were constructed by Claude Tiblier. It was not until the 1920s that "Count" Arnaud Cazenave, the founder (in 1918) of Arnaud's Restaurant in the French Quarter (813 Bienville), removed the common wall and combined both buildings to form the present structure with its imposing Italianate entrance. It remained in the Arnaud family until 1983. The building sat vacant for a few years until Canadian Daniel Lanois, the Grammy-winning musician and music producer, acquired it in 1989 and established Kingsway, a twelve-thousand-square-foot state-of-the-art recording studio, but with classic, vintage equipment. The studio was downstairs, and there were six private bedroom suites upstairs that allowed the musicians to stay in-house. Kingsway produced albums by local musicians such as the Neville Brothers, Zachary Richard, the Iguanas and, either all or in part, albums by Bob Dylan, Pearl Jam, REM, Emmylou Harris, Sheryl Crow, Chris Whitley, Iggy Pop, and the Afghan Whigs, among others. In 1999, Lanois put the building up for sale for $2.4 million. In 2002, Nicolas Cage bought the building and lived in it briefly until it was foreclosed upon. The property is presently owned by developer Sean Cummings and used for special events.

## 534–36 ESPLANADE (CIRCA 1900)

This inset late Victorian two story with a deep balcony on the second floor built by the Vaccaro Brothers was originally a two-family dwelling with a common wall. It was converted into four rental units probably in the early 1940s. In the 1970s, the two lower apartments were combined by the new owner, retaining two rentals.

## 524 ESPLANADE (1846), WEYSHAM-RONSTROM HOUSE

L. Herman Weysham built this masonry structure, and it remains a classic example of the few remaining center-hall buildings with double parlors on either side, kitchen in the back and bedrooms on the second floor. When he died in 1849, the house passed into the Barjac family until 1893. As late as 1939, when the Ronstoms acquired it, it had no electricity or indoor plumbing.

## 510 ESPLANADE

This lot was originally part of the parcel extending to Decatur, the next cross street. The lots were broken up and had multiple owners, several living abroad. Around 1884, this lot was owned by the Nami family, who also owned the corner buildings fronting on Decatur, where they operated a well-known jewelry store. In February 1924, John Dos Passos, broke, moved down to New Orleans from Brooklyn Heights to complete work on his major novel, *Manhattan Transfer* (1925). He paid $2.50/week for his accommodations on the second floor. After a month, he wrote to a friend in New York City: "New Orleans suits me to a T. I don't know anyone so I live cheap and work continuously…It's a fine town…full of noise and jingle and horse racing and crap shooting and whoring and bawdry. Why don't you come down?"

*Cross Decatur Street to the Old U.S. Mint*

## 400 ESPLANADE (1835), OLD U.S. MINT

The northeastern edge of the French Quarter was the site of two fortifications preceding the construction of the Mint: a ditch to fend off attacks from the Natchez (1731) and a wooden palisade (circa 1760) erected around the city for fear of an attack by the British, who had defeated the French in Canada and were threatening the whole Mississippi Valley. On the corner nearest the Mississippi River, an elevated stockade was erected called Fort Saint Charles. When the Spanish came in, the outer area was retrenched and the stockade refortified and renamed Fort San Carlos (1792). By 1804, at the time of the Louisiana Purchase, all the defenses had collapsed from decay and neglect and were torn down. Although in dilapidated condition, Fort Saint Charles survived, and it was from here that Jackson reviewed his troops marching off to the Chalmette battlefield. By 1821, it was demolished, and a public area named variously, Jackson Place/Park/Square commemorated his victory.

"The U.S. Mint and Esplanade Ave., c. 1880–1901." *Library of Congress.*

In the 1830s, New Orleans, now the fifth-largest city in the United States and some say the richest, was fast becoming the commercial emporium of the country. Between 1836 and 1843, New Orleans exported more than New York City—and a considerable amount of Mexican gold flowed into the city. It was an appropriate place to locate a branch of the U.S. Federal Mint, to relieve the pressure on the Philadelphia Mint and to provide money for western expansion. Anyone could bring gold dust, jewelry or foreign coins for assay and conversion to U.S. coins.

Construction was authorized by an act of Congress on March 3, 1835. William Strickland laid out the plans for an E-shaped, three-story building, a masterpiece of grace and severity; however, he neglected to visit the construction site and did not take into consideration the marshy soil. James Gallier Sr. was called in to shore up the sinking building. Minting began officially in 1838. Further repairs to the roof and fireproofing were carried out between 1856 and 1859 by P.G.T. Beauregard, who had graduated from West Point as a civil engineer. At this time, the hand presses were replaced with a steam engine for which a smokestack at the back of the building was erected.

The Mint continuously produced all the coinage in use, both silver and gold, from the three-cent piece to the twenty-dollar double eagle, with occasional operational suspensions for yellow fever outbreaks. On January 26, 1861, when Louisiana seceded from the Union, the state took over the Mint on behalf of the Confederacy. The Confederacy continued to mint regular coinage through April 1861, until the bullion ran out. New half-dollar dies had been cast with the Confederate coat of arms on the reverse, but there was, purportedly, only enough metal to strike four coins. While there were re-strikes made later, it is probable that the existence of these original four coins is entirely mythical.

In April 1862, New Orleans was captured and occupied by Union troops under the command of Benjamin "Beast" Butler. A Stars and Stripes hoisted over the Mint was torn down in an act of minor defiance by William Mumford, but Butler promptly hanged him in the Mint's back courtyard on Barracks Street—an act that Lord Palmerston, the British prime minister, thought barbarous and which caused Jefferson Davis to threaten Butler with hanging on sight.

In 1879, the federal government reactivated the Mint with new equipment, and it minted mostly half dollars and the famed Morgan dollar. When it was finally shut down in 1909, the Mint had produced silver and gold coins worth $249 million and $48 million, respectively. It is estimated that only 2 to 4 percent of these coins exist today.

From 1909 to 1932, the building served as an assay office and, until 1943, as a federal prison, mostly for all the Prohibition violators in New Orleans. It was at this time that the smokestack was taken down. The U.S. Coast Guard used the Mint until 1948 as a recruiting and training station. In July 1965, the federal government tried to sell it but got no acceptable bids and decided to demolish it instead. The state stepped in, acquired the building and, between 1978 and 1980, made extensive renovations to accommodate exhibitions and archival storage. During Katrina's hurricane-force winds, more than 65 percent of the copper cladding on the Mint's roof curled off, but there was only minimal damage to the collection. Since 1981, the Mint has been part of the Louisiana State Museum complex and houses the New Orleans Jazz Museum and a Newcomb Pottery exhibit, schedules regular musical performances and is the home base for the Satchmo Summerfest every August. (U.S. Mint information, 504-568-6993)

*Head back toward Jackson Square*

Walking past the Mint on Esplanade toward the river, take a right on North Peters, alongside the Mint, to head back to Jackson Square. At Barracks Street, to the right, are the courtyards of the Old Mint, where Mumford was hanged. Farther up North Peters, on the right, is the Community Flea Market, which dates its origins to the trinket and household knickknack peddlers in the area in the 1850s, and the Farmers' and Vegetable Market, which began on this site in 1822. At the tip of the triangle of the Vegetable Market, where North Peters merges with Decatur, is the tiny Place de France Park and the golden statue of Saint Joan of Arc, the Maid of Orleans. In 1958, World House in New York City acquired the foundry in Paris where the statue was in storage, one of eight or ten castings from

"French Market, c. 1906." *Library of Congress.*

the original commissioned from the sculptor, Emmanuel Frémiet, by Napoleon III in 1875. The owner of World House consigned it to New Orleans, but the city could not budget the $35,000 to purchase it. It sat in storage until Charles de Gaulle and the Cities of Orleans, Paris, Rheims and Rouen raised the money and gave the statue to New Orleans as "A Gift from the French People" in 1964.

After the city had prepared the site at the foot of Canal Street, the statue was dedicated in October 1972. It was re-gilded in 1984. When it was apparent that the construction of Harrah's Casino would encroach on the site, the statue was relocated in 1999 to its present location. On January 6 of every year, on Joan of Arc's birthday (and coincidently, Twelfth Night, the beginning of the Mardi Gras season), the Krewe de Jeanne d'Arc parades from the statue of Bienville, on Decatur and Conti Streets, to Place de France to celebrate the honorary patron saint of New Orleans and the historical bond between France and New Orleans.

121

"Begue's Exchange." Madam Begue's restaurant. *Library of Congress.*

*Glance across the street*

## 832 DECATUR (1830)

Before Tujacque's Restaurant moved here in 1921, Madam Begué's had been located there since 1850. She was famous among the dockworkers and tourists for the monstrous breakfasts that would keep a customer eating at his table continuously from morning through afternoon. Miss Elizabeth Kettering came from Bavaria to join her brother in New Orleans in 1853. She married Louis Dutrey, who had a coffee and toddy shop in this location. It was Mrs. Dutrey's breakfasts that brought the café fame. When Dutrey died in 1875, she married Hypolite Begué, a butcher who specialized in carving steaks, in 1880. A few years later, the restaurant became Madam Begué's.

"Italian Headquarters, Madison Street, c. 1906." *Library of Congress.*

## THE ITALIAN QUARTER

Madison is the short street next to Madam Bequé's. At the turn of the twentieth century, the French Quarter was, more properly, the Italian Quarter. In all likelihood, the "headquarters" was there to help settle newly arrived immigrants, mostly from Sicily. It certainly was a place to report any acts of discrimination and to function as an "anti-defamation" office. Just fifteen years earlier, on March 1, 1891, the shooting of Police Chief David Hennessey had caused the arrest of about nineteen Italian suspects. Eleven of them were tried and acquitted for lack of evidence, much to the disgust of the citizenry who suspected jury tampering. On March 14, a mob formed, stormed the jail and brutally shot and killed eleven defenseless men—grotesquely, two of the men, one mortally wounded and the other one dead, were hauled outside and hanged. Eight of the men escaped. The story was international news, and the term "Mafia" entered the general vocabulary. The Italian government was so infuriated that it broke off diplomatic relations

123

and threatened military action against the United States. In April 1892, the U.S. government paid an indemnity of $25,000 to the Italian government for the families of those murdered.

### BEER, JAZZ AND LADIES OF THE NIGHT

Farther down Decatur, on that same side of the street, toward Esplanade Avenue, in the 1000 and 1100 blocks, especially in the row houses behind the Ursuline Convent, there were located numerous beer joints in the 1920s and '30s, like the Popeye, the King Fish, Charlie Palooka's, the Black Cat and Heavey's Seventh Heaven, and they were all centers for hot food and hot jazz.

The early histories of New Orleans jazz and prostitution have been inextricably linked. There was, however, a lot more prostitution in the old days than there was jazz. It is unlikely, as some have suggested, that there was a whorehouse on of every single block of the French Quarter (they are the same ones who suggest all those whorehouses have now been replaced by lawyers' offices). In actuality, while there may have been independent operators, there were always unofficial red-light districts in and around the French Quarter. The first, though, was probably a sizable area on the other side of Canal Street in what is now the CBD, called "The Swamp," located between Girod and Julia Streets and the Superdome. It was in full sway from about 1820 to 1850 or so—an area of canvas tents, derelict houses used as sleazy boardinghouses and live music dance halls. It was a section so deadly that no civic ordinances could bring it under control.

The French Quarter had Smokey Row on the 300 block of Burgundy, between Conti and Bienville, which advertised more than one hundred black women of every size and age. Since law forbid them from soliciting in the street, as the story goes, they would reach out from the window and grab the hat off a passerby, obliging him to come in to retrieve it and perhaps stay awhile.

The Swamp and Smokey Row both declined under the impact of Galatin Street, which was in this part of the lower French Quarter. The location of Galatin Street is a matter of dispute. Some argue it was the few blocks on Barracks Street, behind the U.S. Mint, between North Peters and Chartres Street; others (and this is more likely) claim it was three or four blocks upriver from Barracks Street alongside the Mississippi River. It is probable that it spilled over to both areas in question. Hovels, "cribs," saloons, gambling joints and live music dance halls—so dangerous that the police never set foot there unless in force. It didn't help matters that an Irish gang, the Live Oak Boys, contributed to the mayhem, setting fires and clubbing business owners and clients alike, or that some of the whores in residence were named Black Sophie, One-Eyed Red-Light Liz, Mary Jane "Bricktop" Jackson (a redhead who killed at least four men) and America Williams (who billed herself as "the world strongest whore"). Under severe civic pressure, the area was demolished utterly in the 1890s to make way for the expansion and renovation of the French Market.

The city decided it needed to get control of prostitution, and in 1897, Sidney Story, a city alderman, sponsored a resolution that would confine prostitution to an eighteen-block area around Basin Street, just outside the French Quarter. The alderman's name became forever attached to the famous Storyville district, the first official red-light district in the United States. It was a more orderly area, with gaudy mansions with posh interiors, honky-tonks, gambling joints and dance halls with live jazz. The "tenderloin" district even had its own guides—the *Green Book*, *The Lid*, *Hell-o*, *The Sporting Guide* and the famous *Blue Book*, where each madam could extol her establishment and her girls under the headings "White" and "Colored." However, President Woodrow Wilson's Navy Department decided Storyville was distracting young sailors from their patriotic duties during World War I, and a local ordinance shut down Storyville on October 10, 1917. But for two decades, black and white musicians played side-by-side, perfecting the genius of jazz and preparing it for export to Chicago and New York City.

*Cross Decatur Street and head toward the river*

"Oyster Luggers at New Orleans, c. 1906." In these flat-bottomed boats, elsewhere called "Skipjacks," the oyster men would bring their haul to the French Market, near Barracks Street. Evidenced by the long poles, with rake-like ends, or "tongs," they did not dredge but rather poked around and could bring up ten or twenty oysters at once. *Library of Congress.*

"The French Market c. 1900." *Library of Congress.*

"A corner of the French Market, c. 1900–1910." *Library of Congress.*

## THE FRENCH MARKET

Walking up Decatur Street, on the river side, the enclosed shop area on the left was once an open space near the bank of the river where the larger tribal groups, like the Choctaw and Chickasaw, and the smaller groups, like the Chitimacha, the Tunica and the Houmas, living on the outskirts along the bayous would all come and spread blankets to sell herbs, firewood, reed cane baskets and freshly killed game to the colonials. The Spanish enclosed the market around 1782, and the Americans added a meat market and additional buildings after 1813. The market flourished throughout the nineteenth century, despite hurricanes and fires, but by the turn of the century, the buildings had become increasingly dilapidated. In the late 1930s, the WPA stepped in and added extensive and permanent structures. By this time, however, most of the vendors had moved to the area of the Farmers' Market now conventionally called The French Market. That area became totally commercialized

127

by the city's remodeling in 1974 and an overrun, fraught $7.2 million "restoration" in 2006–09—the French Market is not, as it was in 1821, all mud and cypress driftwood and Indian blankets when John James Audubon would come by to collect bird carcasses to take to his nearby studio at 706 Barracks Street to study and paint.

Up ahead, once again, is the green- and white-striped canopy of Café du Monde, the oldest tenant of the original French Market. It's time for another café au lait with chicory and a plate of beignets. The view of Jackson Square is appropriate—where history penetrates into the present so elegantly: "The past is never dead. It's not even past." When Faulkner wrote that line, he could have been thinking back to his days in the French Quarter.

# Bibliography

Anonymous. *New Orleans Courtyards and Gardens*. Los Angeles: Knapp Press, 1984.

———. *New Orleans Decorative Ironwork*. Los Angeles: Knapp, 1984.

Antippas, Andy P. "Creme de Mint." *New Orleans Magazine* 10, no. 2 (November 1975): 66–70.

———. "A Walk Down Royal Street." *New South* (October 1982): 42–43.

Asbury, Herbert. *The French Quarter: An Informal History of the New Orleans Underworld*. New York: Alfred A. Knopf, 1936.

Blount, Roy, Jr. *Feet on the Street: Rambles Around New Orleans*. New York: Crown, 2005.

Cable, George W. "Clarisse Délicieuse." In *Old Creole Days*. New York: Heritage Press, 1943.

Cable, Mary. *Lost New Orleans*. Boston: Houghton Mifflin, 1980.

Campanella, Richard, and Marina Campanella. *New Orleans Then and Now.* Gretna, LA: Pelican, 1999.

Christovich, May Louise, et al. *The Esplanade Ridge.* Vol. V, *New Orleans Architecture.* Gretna, LA: Pelican, 1977.

Clisby, Arthur Stanley, ed. *Susan Cole Doré: Old New Orleans.* Gretna, LA: Pelican, 1936, 1990.

Cowan, Walter G., et al. *New Orleans: Yesterday and Today: A Guide to the City.* Baton Rouge: Louisiana State University Press, 1983.

Delehanty, Randolph. *Ultimate Guide to New Orleans.* San Francisco: Chronicle Books, 1998.

Eco, Umberto. *Travels in Hyperreality.* Translated by William Weaver. Orlando, FL: Harcourt Brace and Company, 1986.

Guillory, Monique. "Under One Roof: The Sins and Sanctity of the New Orleans Quadroon Balls." In *Race Consciousness: African American Studies for the New Century*, pp. 76–92, edited by Judith J. Fossett and Jeffrey Tucker. New York: New York University Press, 1997.

Huber, Leonard V. *Baroness Pontalba's Buildings.* New Orleans: New Orleans Chapter of the Louisiana Landmarks Society and Friends of the Cabildo, 1964.

———. *The Basilica in Jackson Square: The History of the St. Louis Cathedral and Its Predecessors, 1727–1965.* New Orleans, LA: St Louis Cathedral, 1972.

———. *New Orleans: A Pictorial History.* New York: Crown, 1971.

Jewell, Edwin L. *Jewell's Crescent City, Illustrated.* Edited by Edwin L. Jewell. New Orleans, LA: Edwin L. Jewell, 1874.

Kendall, John Smith. *History of New Orleans*. 3 vols. Chicago: Lewis Publishing Co., 1922.

King, Grace. *History of the Creole Families of New Orleans*. New York: Macmillan, 1921.

Love, Victoria C., and Shannon Lorelei. *Mad Madame LaLaurie*. Charleston, SC: The History Press, 2011.

Malone, Lee, and Paul Malone. *The Majesty of New Orleans*. Gretna, LA: Pelican, 1992.

Martin, Francis-Xavier. *The History of Louisiana from the Earliest Period*. 2 vols. Gretna, LA: Pelican, (1921) 2000.

McCaffety, Kerri. *The Majesty of the French Quarter*. Gretna, LA: Pelican, 1999.

Nystrom, Justin A. *New Orleans after the Civil War: Race, Politics, and a New Birth of Freedom*. Baltimore, MD: Johns Hopkins University Press, 2010.

Reed, John Shelton. *Dixie Bohemia: A French Quarter Circle in the 1920s*. Baton Rouge: Louisiana State University, 2012.

Rose, Al. *Storyville, New Orleans*. Birmingham: University of Alabama Press, 1978.

Saxon, Lyle, ed. *Fabulous New Orleans*. New York: Appleton Century Co., 1928.

———. *FWP: New Orleans City Guide*. Boston: Houghton Mifflin, 1938.

Schaefer, Judith Kelleher. *Brothels, Depravity, and Abandoned Women: Illegal Sex in Antebellum New Orleans*. Baton Rouge: Louisiana State University Press, 2009.

Semple, Henry Churchill. *The Ursulines in New Orleans, and Our Lady of Prompt Succor: A Record of Two Centuries, 1727–1925.* New York: P.J. Kennedy, 1925.

Souther, Jonathan Mark. *New Orleans on Parade: Tourism and the Transformation of the Crescent City.* Baton Rouge: Louisiana State University Press, 2006.

Stanonis, Anthony. *Creating the Big Easy: New Orleans and the Emergence of Modern Tourism, 1918–1945.* Athens: University of Georgia Press, 2006.

Tallant, Robert. *Louisiana: A History.* New York: Norton, 1984.

———. *The Romantic New Orleanians.* New York: Dutton, 1950.

Taylor, Troy. *Haunted New Orleans.* Charleston, SC: The History Press, 2010.

———. *Wicked New Orleans: The Dark Side of the Big Easy.* Charleston, SC: The History Press, 2010.

Toledano, Roulhac. *The National Trust Guide to New Orleans.* New York: Preservation Press, 1996.

Wilson, Samuel, Jr. *A Guide to Architecture of New Orleans, 1699–1959.* New York: Reingold Publishing, 1959.

# Index

# About the Author

A ndy P. Antippas, a former associate professor of nineteenth-century English literature, is the owner and director of Barrister's Gallery in New Orleans since 1976. He has lived and worked in the French Quarter for thirty years.